a Version of the Truth

Marsh Rose

Mechanicsburg, PA USA

Published by Sunbury Press, Inc.
Mechanicsburg, Pennsylvania

www.sunburypress.com

Copyright © 2025 by Marsh Rose.
Cover Copyright © 2025 by Sunbury Press, Inc.

Sunbury Press supports copyright. Copyright fuels creativity, encourages diverse voices, promotes free speech, and creates a vibrant culture. Thank you for buying an authorized edition of this book and for complying with copyright laws by not reproducing, scanning, or distributing any part of it in any form without permission. You are supporting writers and allowing Sunbury Press to continue to publish books for every reader. For information contact Sunbury Press, Inc., Subsidiary Rights Dept., PO Box 548, Boiling Springs, PA 17007 USA or legal@sunburypress.com.

For information about special discounts for bulk purchases, please contact Sunbury Press Orders Dept. at (855) 338-8359 or orders@sunburypress.com.

To request one of our authors for speaking engagements or book signings, please contact Sunbury Press Publicity Dept. at publicity@sunburypress.com.

FIRST SUNBURY PRESS EDITION: August 2025

Set in Adobe Garamond | Interior design by Crystal Devine | Cover by Angeleen Hill | Edited by Lucia Monte.

Publisher's Cataloging-in-Publication Data
Names: Rose, Marsh, author.
Title: A version of the truth / Marsh Rose.
Description: First trade paperback edition. | Mechanicsburg, PA : Sunbury Press, 2025.
Summary: A Version Of the Truth follows the evolution of a relationship that spans almost forty years and ends with some universal questions. What does it mean to truly know another person, and how do we find truth when life gives us unsolvable mysteries?
Identifiers: ISBN : 979-8-88819-325-9 (paperback).
Subjects: BIOGRAPHY & AUTOBIOGRAPHY / Memoirs | BIOGRAPHY & AUTOBIOGRAPHY / Women | FAMILY & RELATIONSHIPS / Love & Romance.

Designed in the USA
0 1 1 2 3 5 8 13 21 34 55

For the Love of Books!

Disclaimer

A Version of the Truth is a true story, but to ensure anonymity and protect privacy, I have changed the names of all individuals and locations mentioned here. There is no town called Vineyard View in California.

Acknowledgments

Words can never express my gratitude for the support of authors Carol Costello and Marion Roach Smith, great friends who stayed with me over the months while the memoir took form in writing, and in life as the ending of the story unfolded. Their patience, humor, and commitment were inspirational.

Of course, once again, as always, vast appreciation for the talent and expertise of the extraordinary Sunbury Press staff: Dr. Lawrence Knorr, publisher; Nicole Brown, assistant publisher, Lucia Monte, editor; Angeleen Hill, book cover artist; John Jordan, marketing and publicity; Crystal Devine, design.

Thanks to the team at Books Forward: E.W. Martin, executive administrator; Corrine Pritchett, publicist and digital marketing.

And a round of applause for my tribe of writers, artists, authors and readers: Wynne Bergman, Kathy Brownback, Jabez Churchill, Margi Haas, Joan Hocky, Jo Lauer, Taryn Mirabello, Rachel Moore, Susan Pervis, Dana Sivula, Rick Speas, Paul Storm, Patrice Vecchione, Erika Wasser.

Chapter One

"You live in this miserable heap all by yourself."
—A Strange Man

What would you do if you needed the answer to an usnsolvable mystery? Would you drive yourself mad, searching? Would you cling to denial while it paced the edges of your awareness? Or would you get a version you could live with, and live with it? Jack and I were in an intimate relationship for almost forty years. While we never married or shared a home, we spent two nights a week together and talked on the phone almost every day. He saw me through houses, cars, careers, pets, crises, and celebrations. And then, he vanished. When I found him ten days later, he'd had a hemorrhagic stroke. He was incapacitated. He could no longer speak. His memory was lost. And he was living with another woman who called him by a different name.

We met in 1985. I was 35 and he was 40. He turned up at the door of my decrepit rental in the rural Northern California town where I had just moved from Philadelphia. I'd had a bad night. Although I was an urban transplant, I was no stranger to wild animals. Feral cats wandering the streets at night in Philly would awaken me with their shrieks, and we had the occasional rat in our trash, and mouse in the pantry. Once, a bat got into the attic and my father caught it in a pillowcase while Mom and I cowered in a closet. Those creatures were tame compared to the menagerie that circled my country bungalow when the sun went down. I heard scrabbling and squalling from the underbrush, saw eyeshine in the hedges. In the morning I counted tracks in the mud, all sizes and shapes of tracks, any number of toes, something that slithered and something with opposable thumbs that I hoped to hell was a raccoon. A monkey would have sent me over the edge. I was in a state of anxiety-fueled insomnia. Animals made me nervous. You can't tell what they're thinking. Fear of animals is an actual thing. Zoophobia. I learned about it in graduate school when I was working on my degree in clinical psychology. "An intense, irrational, and uncontrollable fear of animals." So, to scare them away, that night I had turned on every light in the house, inside and out, including a spotlight over the back porch.

Someone rang my doorbell the next morning. There was no peephole for me to see who had come calling, so against my urban instincts, I opened the door. For one brilliant moment, I thought the man standing on my porch was my high school crush, Jimmy Lee Bevins. That shaggy auburn hair, those wide blue eyes, the tattered blue jeans, the cowboy boots. I was in love with Jimmy Lee, and he with . . . well, officially with Joanne Malloy but probably with any of the hardened girls who chewed gum with their mouths open and smoked behind the bleachers. Jimmy Lee never knew I existed: the small, skinny sophomore with frizzy hair and thick glasses. And now, here was his adult doppelganger casting a long shadow over my front porch.

"I seen your lights on all night," the man said. "What's the matter?"

The only other residence on this isolated cul-de-sac was a ragged farmhouse. I noted it warily each time I passed. It looked like news images of Barker Ranch where Charles Manson gathered his followers: a one-story frame house, a barn with a collapsing roof, a collection of vehicles, and donkeys or horses or some other large animal in a dusty pasture.

I peered past the man and saw no car in my driveway. Had he too been lurking in the bushes last night? My voice in my ears sounded an octave higher than normal. "Who are you and how did you know my lights were on?"

"Oh, sorry. Name's Jack." He held out his right hand. I reflexively shook it, noting the warmth and calluses that felt like sandpaper. "I live up there." He pointed toward the farmhouse. Having shaken hands, the moment for me to slam the door had passed. "I was worried. Usually, the only reason for lights to be on all night is someone is up sick. And you live in this miserable heap all by yourself."

What to do? On one hand, he knew I lived alone, and he could be a cult leader. On the other hand, I was in the nostalgic haze of Jimmie Lee. That's how it began.

Chapter Two

*"Goddamn hippies! Dress like witch doctors!
Fornicate like rabbits!"*
—My landlord

I never would have settled for that rented shanty, but I was desperate for a roof over my head. It was my fault. When I came out from Philly, it was to accept a dream job as a psychotherapist in an addiction treatment facility and I hadn't bothered to research the cost of housing in the north San Francisco Bay area. It evidently equaled that of the French Riviera, while my finances were barely equal to the monthly $300 fee for a 700-square-foot bungalow. According to rumor, it was affordable only because of a town law, implemented by a progressive young city council, that infuriated local landlords. Rent control. It prohibited property owners from raising rent unless there was a structural crisis, and only after navigating a bureaucratic thicket. Landlords in other towns would have asked triple that amount for the same hovel. My new landlord, Earl, owner of the auto repair shop, did not think kindly of the law.

"Rent control! Goddamn hippies!" he thundered. "Dress like witch doctors! Fornicate like rabbits!" Since we had met only moments earlier on the rickety front porch and I would spend my fifth night in my car if I couldn't land this place, I nodded and smiled and tucked my hand into my pocket to hide my wrist tattoo of a feather. At the time, the only women I knew of who had tattoos were the late Janis Joplin, and Cher. "It's socialism," he shouted. "We might as well have lost the war!" I didn't know which war he meant, but this wasn't the time to ask. "Now you take your renters." I waited. "I had these renters in here two, three years back? They move in and right away they're camped out on my doorstep." He affected a whining falsetto. "'Oh Earl, your bungalow is so drafty. It makes my camel meal tea get cold.'" I saw a visual image of renters from Saudi Arabia camped on his doorstep in their traditional keffiyehs, sipping their "camel meal tea."

"It took me two hours to caulk the windows," he continued. "I make a repair like that, I gotta raise the rent. That means filling out forms with those scum-suckers at the Rent Control Board. They coulda caulked the goddamned windows themselves but no, guess they'd rather pay me $50 more a month."

I got the point. A call to Earl would mean a rent increase I couldn't afford.

We walked through the front door. The bungalow's floors seemed spongy, and I smelled the sharp odorous signatures of cats and mice. Mildew patches stained the walls. The bathroom's linoleum showed barren patches, and the bedroom carpet was worn through to bare planks. The living room reminded me of a gangster's hideout. There was a lumpy sofa, a recliner with grimy armrests and a scarred coffee table. All it needed to complete the ambiance were Mafioso in shiny suits, crouched on the floor behind the couch, peering through the curtains. With no other options, I resignedly accepted a rental agreement and Earl roared off down the driveway in a tow truck and a plume of dust.

I learned that I could take a reasonable shower in the morning if I didn't use hot water after 5 P.M. the night before, that the use of any two electrical devices at the same time would blow a fuse, and that something somewhere in the bungalow intermittently made a sound like a jet plane. Along with the marauding animals, that was the state of things when Jack materialized on my doorstep.

"How are you making out in this place?" he asked after our brief introduction at the door.

"Not well. I'm freezing. The windows are closed so I don't know where the cold air is coming from. I should have moved to that place they call California."

"Beach Boys, surfers, people lying on sand under umbrellas?"

"Yes, that sort of thing."

"That's Southern California. Different world. You can't lay out on beaches here. You'd get sandblasted by the wind. Speaking of wind, your problem here is, your front door needs rehanging. Look at this damned thing. You got a gap you could drive a truck through."

"Do I have to tell Earl?"

"No, you have to tell me. I'm a construction worker. Earl's a good guy but he works about a million hours a day and he doesn't always take care of things."

So, Jack rehung the door. He wouldn't accept payment. "Neighbors don't pay each other," he said. To thank him, I offered to make dinner. I thought he looked hungry.

Making dinner might not have been the best idea. Friends invite me to their potlucks on the condition that I not bring a homemade dish. "Just stop at the 7-11," they say. "Get something in a shiny bag. Don't open it." Every time, despite my vows to curb my impatience, when I cook, I cut corners, skip steps, and tell myself that the stuff is all going to end up in the same place anyway so why bother with more than one pot and spoon? But I wanted to impress Jack with a simple, tasty, nutritious dish and I knew a culinary artist whose rich commands of flavor and aroma would wow a French chef. She could direct me. In fact, I had her on speed-dial.

"Mom? How do you make spaghetti?"

"What, you're turning Italian? Why don't you make him some nice beef stroganoff, something from your own people?"

"Well, I . . . wait. How do you know I'm cooking for a man?"

"The day you cook spaghetti for yourself is the day I pass out from shock and I'm hosting Mah Jong in an hour. And all the women you know don't eat any more than you do. God forbid you should all swell up to a size two." This was a long-standing argument about a forbidden issue. My weight. It's normal. I'm 5' tall and I've weighed 100 pounds since high school, a condition my mother views as anorexic. Mom went on. "When is the dinner and what do you have for ingredients?"

"Tomorrow night, and some garlic salt."

"Oy gevalt. Get a can of Hunt's ready-to-eat spaghetti sauce . . ."

After Jack rehung the door, he fixed the furnace, replaced a leaking water line, changed the fuses, re-wired the kitchen light and patched a hole in the porch where the termites had eaten through. I ordered Chinese takeout and pizza delivery so often, I had them on speed-dial too.

Chapter Three

"I'm like an old dog."
—Jack

We never should have been in any room together, much less naked in my bedroom six months and a long list of bungalow repairs later. We were incompatible. He was country, born and raised on the farm he inherited when his parents died. I was city. He claimed that a tenth-grade education had never slowed him down. I had trudged through the requisite years of schooling and licensure needed to practice psychotherapy. Where he was easygoing, I confronted. He hoarded, I discarded. He could look out at the world and see exactly how everything should fit together, and if it didn't fit together, how to fix it. I felt more comfortable with thoughts and feelings. True, they were invisible and difficult to understand but not as difficult as understanding why the lights in the bungalow flickered every time I flushed the toilet.

His ancestors came from Norway, the people who gave him those long legs and high cheekbones, pale skin and red-gold hair. My recent bloodline extends back to the Russian and Hungarian Jews who flooded Ellis Island in the 1930s. And according to family legend, also flowing through my veins is a soupçon of Mongol blood which explains my wild hair and olive complexion. Jack said he was probably in a Protestant church as a child, but he didn't recall. My family didn't observe traditional religious rituals, but we were appropriately subdued for the High Holidays—Rosh Hashana and, seven days later, Yom Kippur—and we ate and danced and sang on Passover and Hannukah and Purim.

Jack and I didn't even listen to the same music. He once confused Janis Joplin with Linda Ronstadt, and I can't tell the difference between Willie Nelson and the guy who sings "Bubba Shot the Jukebox."

However, for all the ways we didn't match, we did share profound needs for privacy and independence while still craving intimacy. When I left Philly, I left behind a long-term relationship with a university professor whose interest in his teaching assistant had eclipsed his interest in me. After him and until Jack, the only man whose company I desired was famed British naturalist, David Attenborough. My vast collection of his nature documentaries were the first things I unpacked in the bungalow, along with my VCR. The satire didn't escape me. I was terrified of small creatures in the shrubbery, while in my fantasies I loved a man who could pet the wild lemur that was blowing in his ear.

Despite my Baby Boomer generation, I don't believe in past lives or other New Age theories. If I felt I had always known Jack, maybe he used the same soap as Jimmy Lee Bevins. Maybe that scent rang a chime in my hippocampus, the tiny organ in our brains that connects emotional memory with sense of smell. Everything can be explained scientifically, even my visceral pull to Jack that made no logical sense but caused me to feel, in his company, like an orbiting planet.

Of course I asked him. He was not married. He never would be, not again. "I'm done with all that crap. Married at twenty, divorced five years later, I learned my lesson. My daddy said you only fall in love once, so I shot my wad. You'll be a special friend but that's all you'll ever be. I'm like an old dog. I'll stay up on the back porch until you try to put a leash on me. If you can't handle it, well . . ." (Here he made a hat-tipping gesture of farewell.)

Since I was afraid of dogs and didn't know how they acted, the exact analogy was lost on me, but I knew he was telling the truth. He was my neighbor. I had been to his farmhouse when he welded a handle on my teakettle. No woman would live under those circumstances. I had never seen an obsessive-compulsive passion like his, and I'm a therapist. His fixation on motorcycles permeated his home and everything in it. When he broke the land speed record at the Bonneville Salt Flat races in Utah in 1983, it was on a Harley-Davidson he had built himself, in his living room where the only furniture was an office chair on wheels. The rest were work benches, milling machines, torque wrenches, and a bookshelf of airplane manuals. The bathroom was unfriendly, and he ate take-out warmed in a microwave. The stove was used for heating various metals.

In contrast with his farm, the bungalow was nearly palatial. So, under its leaking roof, we evolved a routine of getting together after work on Tuesday and Friday nights. We ate, had sex, watched TV and snoozed and sometimes he spent the night. In between dinner and sex, he fixed things. Usually they were things I once thought no mere mortal could fix. Electricity, plumbing, things that needed different screws and other things that needed a variety of nails. He also taught me to fix things. Eventually my drafty pantry held a tool kit well-stocked with overflow from Jack's farm. I could identify the Phillips-head screwdriver. "It's used for tightening those screws with the X on top. And that's a wrench . . . wait, an adjustable wrench. You use it to turn nuts and bolts . . ." He mentored me through my first authentic DIY project, fixing a leak in the toilet tank. We began with a trip to the hardware store for a replacement flapper valve.

Our time together was fun and casual. I would find a real relationship some day and meanwhile, my "special friend" would satisfy my need for intimacy.

For the rest of my waking hours, I was too distracted for serious love-hunting. The clinic was a busy place. We had every variety of addict that could be found in rural America during those years. They came through our doors voluntarily, or it was a last-chance mandate from spouses or parents, or they were sent by the legal system as a condition of probation for some drug-related crime. We had the dreamy heroin users, agitated methamphetamine addicts, pudgy pot smokers, morose alcoholics, sharp-dressing cocaine users and the occasional philosophy-spouting LSD trippers. I was at the office up to ten hours a day.

Then there was the constant dusting and vacuuming in the bungalow, general household and auto requirements, and my social life. That included my cohort of friends, my coworkers, most of whom I liked and admired, and an hour on the phone one Sunday every month with my first cousin Rachel in Toronto. An hour wasn't long enough, given the breadth and depth of convoluted intrigue, gossip and life stories, but long-distance calls were pricey and I wanted to be kept in the loop. I was by default the matriarch of my generation, the eldest of eight cousins on my father's side and the only American. The rest of that close-knit clan, three generations, were born and raised in Toronto and, except for my father when he married Mom in 1945, nobody ever left.

My social life didn't overlap with Jack's. His friends were local ranchers and farmers, construction workers and mechanics. I met a few of them in my first few years with Jack. Most seemed politically and socially conservative, all were White, Anglo-Saxons who had lived in the area for generations, and most were married with children or divorced with joint custody. Our few encounters reminded me of a fox and a porcupine on a David Attenborough documentary. We circled one another and then quietly backed away. It wasn't that I didn't like them, and they weren't hostile. We were simply foreign to one another.

And time slipped by.

Chapter Four

"What do you think of scallops, sauteed in brown butter?"
—Jack

After five years, my twice-weekly routine with Jack focused on two household objects: the stove and the bed.

We couldn't survive on takeout or my feeble culinary efforts, so Jack opted to cook. Unlike me, that man knew his way around a kitchen. His parents had owned the oldest restaurant in town, *Bev's Soup And Sandwich*, and he'd been pressed into service there as a prep cook after school from the age of 10.

It became a standard scenario on Wednesday and Saturday mornings, after we woke and had coffee, with Jack leaning against the scarred kitchen table, gazing at the ceiling for a moment, tapping a notepad with his pencil, planning the menu for his next visit.

"What do you think of scallops, sauteed in brown butter?" he'd ask. "How about a marinera? Tomatoes are in peak season." Then every Tuesday and Friday after work, with his list in hand, I would shop for ingredients. He grilled a slab of local salmon with a honey glaze. He paired the scallops with steamed, fresh broccoli and sourdough bread. And with a glug of Merlot, he simmered the marinera, made from locally grown San Marzano tomatoes and basil. I hadn't eaten that well since I sat at my mother's table.

He also knew his way around the bedroom. My teenage fantasies of Jimmy Lee Bevins were black-and-white daguerreotypes when compared with the adult technicolor reality of Jack.

I would prompt him for stories about growing up on a farm, how he milked the cows, fed the horse and collected eggs. Before knowing him, if pressed I would have asserted that produce and dairy in the supermarket were issued by way of kindly farmers in clean overalls who lived in a place called The Midwest. So I was horrified by Jack's descriptions of "candling" eggs, holding each egg up to a candlelight to ensure it didn't contain a chick embryo before selling it, potentially to a squeamish customer like me.

He took me to a dairy farm to watch his friend Bert milk the cows.

"And it's real milk?" I asked, as we stood in the barn doorway at what I felt was a safe distance from Bert and a cow that looked larger than they did on television.

"It's real milk. Bert sells it to the dairy processors to be pasteurized. Those three ladies at the fence are waiting their turns. Bert will have them all milked in an hour."

"Where are the male cows?"

"Don't let Bert hear you asking about male cows. He'll die laughing and then I'll have to do the milking. A 'male cow' is a bull."

I was galvanized on the morning Jack took me to feed a neighbor's pig. Perhaps from children's stories, cartoons, inattention and misunderstanding, I thought a pig was a small pink creature with a curly tail, the size of a cocker spaniel. Watching this mottled behemoth lumber across the field toward us was as surreal as if it had been a 300-pound rabbit.

If occasionally I wished for a date on Saturday night, I would remind myself of all the cringe-worthy chores that would come with finding someone to go out with me. All that time-sucking waxing, shaving, curling, plucking. And if Jack never invited me to an Independence Day barbecue or a Christmas buffet with his friends, that was OK. Traditional holidays weren't part of my upbringing. My Canadian-born father and American mother could never decide on which side of the border their loyalties lay. Independence Day and its Canadian counterpart, Boxing Day, were summarily revoked at our house before they began. Canadians and Americans observe Thanksgiving in the same way, but Canadians do it on the second Monday in October. For Americans, of course, it's the last Thursday in November. Mom didn't want to spend two entire days in the kitchen, so that one was out too. Since we didn't observe Christmas anyway, we ignored "The Holidays," and I babysat for neighbors on New Years Eve. I never asked Jack about his traditional celebrations.

My friends were not similarly sanguine about my laissez-faire situation. Didn't I want to know what my "intermittent boyfriend" was up to when he wasn't fixing things, cooking, wowing me with farmyard sights or having sex with me? What about Valentine's Day? My friend Brenda threatened to put on a Groucho Marx nose and a babushka, hide in the underbrush at his house and follow Jack to see where he went.

I talked about him, as women do, not to complain or speculate but to share anecdotes. My friends were more intrigued than amused. They prodded me to speculate about him, about our relationship and where it was going. Allison was especially persistent. She stopped by one Friday night when we were having dinner ("accidentally on purpose," I assumed) and I introduced them. She cornered me the next day at the gym.

"So that was the famous invisible boyfriend," she said.

"He's not my boyfriend. He's a friend, and he was a boy long ago . . . and he is *not* my boyfriend. We just enjoy each other's company."

"Don't you want to know where the two of you will be in a year, five years, your old age?"

Allison's husband had just admitted to an affair and occasional use of cocaine but the issue seemed too emotionally charged to use it as an example of the futility of prediction.

"We're just hanging out," I said. "Asking Jack to tell me where he expects to be in my life when we're both geriatric cases will prompt another 'I'm like an old dog' talk. It's good enough to know where we'll be next Tuesday. The answer is, in my kitchen, having dinner."

Eventually my friends let the matter drop, and I was relieved. I'm sensitive to the onus of my profession. People think therapists walk around analyzing everyone, as if we have a copy of the *Diagnostic and Statistical Manual of Mental Disorders,* "the *DSM,*" etched into our grey matter. I didn't want anyone to think I was using my work skills on Jack.

It wasn't as easy to slip the hook among my colleagues at the clinic. They pressured me to disclose more about my "twice a week man." Surely, he'd accompany me to a staff picnic on Sunday afternoon. No? They prodded, in the classic therapist pose, leaning forward, one hand tucked under the chin, forehead furrowed. Some of their theories fringed on the facetious. Perhaps it was an innovative prison program that allowed inmates to go home, but only on Tuesday and Friday nights? I suspect several really did come up with a DSM diagnosis ... for me.

Chapter Five

"Out, damned spot."
—Shakespeare's Lady Macbeth

By 1995 I had shifted gears professionally, literally, and emotionally.

Professionally, it was logical to move from working with addicts to working with survivors of trauma. Post traumatic stress disorder (PTSD) had finally been recognized as a medical and psychological illness, and I was hired as a psychotherapist at a clinic that treated military combat veterans who suffered from that condition. Some came off the streets by way of the Vietnam War, ragged and ranting and hungry. Some came from the Gulf War. Almost all were addicted to drugs or alcohol, choosing a relief that couldn't be found through talk therapy or prescription medication. Scenes from their stories of battles in Hue or Medina Ridge would replay in my mind, day after day. Sometimes I shared even their nightmares.

Jack had no frame of reference for my work. He had never known someone who sought psychotherapy, much less offered it. Many of his friends were combat veterans and, he said, "there was nothing wrong with them." Still, he knew I was affected, and he kept me laughing and distracted every Tuesday and Friday night with anecdotes about those friends, mischief as a teenager, and calamitous blunders on the construction site. The humor became a balm and balance for the horrors that played out in my inner vision.

And I shifted gears literally. My Honda Civic died after 150,000 miles, and what replacement could be better than a sports car for a single Baby Boomer woman in California? I wanted a ride that would be both fun and affordable, and found a pristine 1970s-era Datsun Z, "The Z-Car," lithe and nimble, easy on the fuel consumption. It had a classic five-speed stick shift, and I had no idea how to operate one, but Jack could teach me. He'd driven a tractor at the age of 14 and had been racing motorcycles since his 20s. In this potentially fraught setting—teaching a grown, stubborn, outspoken woman to drive—he'd be perfect for the job. Reasonable and even-tempered, he would be the opposite of my first driving teacher. Dad. My father behind the wheel was aggressive, as an instructor he was impatient, and he thought I was a wimp. "Get out there," he'd bellow. "Show 'em what you can do!" What I could do was cry and plead to go home. Somehow, I got a driver's license but every car I drove had automatic transmission.

As it turned out, there was an obstacle to my dream of roaring away in the Z with my name on the title. Jack was unavailable.

"I'll be gone for a few weeks," he said.

Gone? Where? Why? I was astonished by the intensity of my reaction. Apparently, while I had been preoccupied with work and the bungalow, my feelings for him had shifted. True, accompanying me to a routine colonoscopy wasn't what I had in mind when I slotted him into that small portion of life I reserved for intimacy, but I wouldn't have asked anyone else. And clearly his feelings had shifted too. When I took him to the hospital for kidney stone surgery, an orderly needed to pry his fingers from my hand before they could wheel him into the operating theater. And now he would be gone? It was time to talk.

Meanwhile, I hired a driving teacher, bought the Z, and when Jack returned, I told him my thoughts. We'd been in an intimate relationship for nearly a decade, yet we never left the bungalow together. He was my neighbor, yet he was invisible for most of the week. We seemed to have gone beyond special friends, yet there was this entrenched schedule. He had met several of my friends, and he knew about my parents and the Toronto gang, yet I was never included in his life beyond hearing the anecdotes. If he wasn't married or in a relationship with someone else, why this veneer of secrecy?

His expression was familiar, one I had seen many times over the course of my life. It mirrored that of my parents. (Why does the sky keep changing colors?) And my seventh-grade teacher. (Why would anyone need algebra?) And, most recently, my driving instructor. (Why do they call it a clutch when we use our foot?) The look was one of mild annoyance and the reminder that it had all been explained before.

"But I told you how it would be when we first got together." He seemed sincerely quizzical. "Nothing changed. I just need my space. I've always been this way, and I always will. I thought you felt the same."

Lately my friends had been alluding to my relationship and the bungalow as two sides of a coin, and that coin was not shiny. A decade is long enough, they chanted. In both heart and home, I was settling for less than I deserved. But, I countered, leave the bungalow? Who would abandon such good fortune as mine? Although rent control had been repealed in 1992, Earl never raised the rent. Month after month I waited for that letter in the mail until Jack explained why it never came. Earl had owned the bungalow for decades. It was surely paid off, the taxes would have been miniscule, and my rent check was basically free money. Earl knew the domino effect. If he demanded more money I would demand improved conditions. Improved conditions would mean a complete remodel with all its complexity and expense. So, he never raised the rent. Because he never raised the rent, I never made demands. And there we hovered, in this delicate unspoken détente while the bungalow continued its inexorable march toward deterioration, and I stockpiled savings against the inevitable need to leave. Jack kept up with the repairs, I tolerated what couldn't be fixed, and my friends and coworkers viewed my nearly rent-free living, $300 a month for a two-bedroom home in pricey "wine country," with combined disbelief and envy.

If I refused to leave the bungalow, they said, at least change my semi-solitary love life. "Get out there!" they cried, eerily echoing my father. So, as the next emotional shift, I resolved to stop waiting for a soulmate and go in search of one, which meant ending my situation with Jack. Sadly, I told him my decision. He accepted with regret but without demur. If I ever needed him, he said, I knew where he was.

I felt seeing him would prompt a slide back into status quo, so for four months I stayed on my end of the road and he stayed on his. I looked up "handyman," "electrician" and "plumber" in the yellow pages and posted their phone numbers on the wall next to those for my doctor and dentist.

Entering the singles scene in the mid-1990s felt like learning to shift gears in a sports car, jarring and unpredictable. I went online but cringed at the feeling of shopping for a human being or marketing myself. So, I enlisted my friends as matchmakers. They fixed me up with a published poet, a computer technician, and a guitarist in a rock band. All were attractive, attentive, and I found fault with each one. He drank too much. He had more baggage than an airline on Thanksgiving. His toes were hairy. His resentful teenage daughter tried to kill me. (She said it was an accident.) But in the end, the underlying truth was always the same. He wanted more of me than I wanted to give. Entire weekends? Unthinkable. Evenings when I wanted to work late? No way. Togetherness that felt like smothering? It made me crabby and withdrawn. Even if there was a spark, I was eager to reclaim my solitude sooner than he was. The guitarist said I always seemed to have one foot out the door.

The Jack embargo was like a stretch in a parched desert. Tuesday and Friday nights were empty. I had never noticed the silence of those little rooms, with only myself and those thoughts of war. David Attenborough and his lemurs could only go so far in assuaging my need for male companionship.

The next shift returned me to where it all began. Wild animals.

Jack had no qualms about using the ancient oven in the bungalow, which had to be lit with a match, but I refused to light it myself. Given the odor of natural gas that permeated the kitchen, I was afraid the appliance might rocket me into the stratosphere. Then one Tuesday evening, craving a hot meal, I walked over to contemplate its menacing porcelain presence and heard a squeak from inside. Oh no. It must be a creature from the underbrush. A mouse, a rat, a possum, a raccoon, what else could be in there? A coyote? I was alone with it. I would never sleep again, much less eat, until it was gone. The remedy was obvious. Chase the creature out into the open and back into the shrubbery. Feeling a thready new sense of competence . . . after all, Jack said I was almost ready to tackle the bungalow's shaky electrical system . . . I opened the bungalow's front door so that the creature, or I, could escape and, broom in hand, I advanced upon the oven.

"Tiny animal, friendly animal," I crooned. Even if it bit me, how much damage could it inflict? I stifled memories of the movie *Old Yeller* when the dog gets rabies, and mental images of myself frothing at the mouth. Keeping up constant silent cheerleading, I yanked open the door, smacked the side of the oven with an opened palm and cried, "out, damned spot!" (Quoting Shakespeare's Lady Macbeth, while illogical, seemed appropriate.) No response. I gritted my teeth, bent down, and looked. I saw nothing in the dark interior but a rusting rack. No nest, no twitching whiskers. I closed the oven door and there it was again—a soft, brief squeak. The creature must have wedged itself inside whatever occult workings lay in an oven. After three loops to the phone and back to the oven,

I called. Jack came. He listened. He opened the oven door, closed it, then stamped his foot. The oven squeaked. He stamped twice. The oven squeaked twice. He tap-danced to the rhythm of "Shave and a Haircut," and the oven squeaked in time.

There was no creature in the oven. The bungalow was built several inches off the ground, he explained, in what he described as a "pillar and post" method, now illegal but typical for houses built in the 1930s in California where there was seldom need for a basement. When I walked across the floor, it would bounce slightly and a rusting hinge on the oven door squeaked. The squeak had always been there, but I hadn't always been anxious and hungry on a silent night when every ambient sound reminded me that I was alone and vulnerable.

"Well, it sounded like an animal," I wailed. "You agree, right? A mouse or a mole or a gopher?"

"It sounded like a rhinoceros. You get a rhino in one of these ovens, the damn things squeak like hell."

And it was back to humor and back to bed and back to dinner and back to the start, with my silent recognition. Whatever accounted for this unavailability, it wasn't a threat to my health or safety. He didn't seem to be doing anything illegal and while his politics listed to the right, I couldn't imagine him kitted out in survival gear, ready to wage war on the government. And it couldn't be a wife or intimate relationship despite the continuing skepticism of my friends. There was no way to convince them without over-disclosing, so I over-disclosed. Jack was nearing 60 by then and still had a robust sexual appetite. A man of his age, in two sexual relationships simultaneously? It could never happen.

Chapter Six

"There are no mice in Philadelphia."
—My Father

My living situation was famous among my social circle, my coworkers, and the Canadians, but there were two people I kept in the dark. They were my loving but chronically bickering, overprotective parents. They knew nothing about the bungalow. I hinted at a charming country cottage with a thatched roof and myself with a wicker basket over my arm, gathering herbs. When I went back to Philly to visit them as I did every few years, we reminisced about my childhood and Dad lectured me about 401k's.

They had disapproved of my move to California. "Why don't you come home?" my father often asked during our monthly phone calls. To my parents, home would always be Philadelphia. "Get a real job instead of working with nut cases out there... Well, whatever they're called. Listen, I play poker with Johnny Street's stockbroker and... what do you mean, who's Johnny Street? He's the mayor of Philadelphia, for chrissake! Anyway, he could open some doors, you could work in an actual office..." Any knowledge of my substandard living situation would prompt them to ramp up their campaign. Add to that my embarrassment about the bungalow, and I was determined to keep them at bay.

They would suggest a visit and I would loop back to my affection for my childhood home, desire to see old friends, paucity of things to do in California, whatever desperate fantasy I could conjure. My ruses were bound to fail eventually, and the tipping point came with a rodent one Sunday morning. We were chatting about their upcoming trip to Hawaii when a mouse skittered across my floor. It startled me. I screamed. They chorused in alarm.

"It's nothing," I said. "It was just a little mouse."

"A mouse! You could get the Black Plague," my mother cried.

"That plague was caused by fleas," my father corrected.

"I don't care what kind of plague she has, rodents are dangerous."

"Calm down," I said. "I live in the country. There are mice."

"There are no mice in Philadelphia," my father announced.

That astonishing claim wasn't worth arguing so I changed the subject, but the mouse matter was far from over.

Two weeks later, while I was trying to wash the kitchen window, delicately, without causing it to catapult out of its frame and into the backyard, I heard voices outside. One was an agitated-sounding male bass, the other a wavering female. I opened the door and once again gaped at the man on my porch. This time it was no time-warp high school Doppelganger. It was my father, scowling up at my sagging rain gutter and thumping on the rotting porch railing. Standing in the yard beside an Avis rental car, looking up at the bungalow as if she feared it would maul her, was my mother, wearing her taupe pantsuit which never wrinkled or showed stains. We all stared for a beat.

"So? You're not going to ask us in?" my father said.

"What the hell . . . what are you doing here? Why didn't you tell me you were coming? You're supposed to be going to Hawaii tomorrow." I frantically cast about in my mind for anything I might have told them about the bungalow.

They followed me into the living room. Mom didn't move her head while her eyes roamed from the threadbare rug to the scarred walls.

"Oh," she said, "we decided to leave a day early so we could stop and see San Francisco. We had to change planes there anyway."

"You said you were changing planes in Denver." They ignored me. Now they were lowering themselves onto the sagging couch, cautiously as if it might explode.

"But it was so foggy you couldn't see your face in front of you," my mother continued, "so we made one of our spontaneous decisions. Since we're in the area, we decided to see you. Silly me, I forgot to bring my phone numbers."

"You've never made a spontaneous decision in your lives, and you know my phone number as well as I do."

My father chimed in. "I need to check the oil in that lemon Avis calls a car." He gave Mom a significant look. "Talk to your daughter." Then he walked out.

Mom smiled at me uncertainly. "I don't like to interfere, but your father hasn't stopped worrying about you. If we asked to see you and you said no, it would hurt his feelings. The doctor told him not to get his blood pressure up."

"And if his blood pressure went up, he'd have a heart attack, and it would be my fault."

"You know how he is. Once he gets his teeth into a problem, he's like a pylori."

"Pylori?"

"Those fish with the teeth. Is there a bathroom here?"

"Piranha. Yes, there's a bathroom. Do you think I pee in the woods? It's down the hall."

She left and my father returned, sat heavily on the couch, crossed his left ankle over his right knee, took a deep breath and exhaled slowly.

" 'Your mother . . . ' " I prompted him.

"Don't be a smartass. She wasn't going to stop with the mouse until I brought her out here. Now I see she was right."

"It's not as bad as it seems," I began when I heard my mother's frightened voice.

"Morrie! There's something wrong in the bathroom!"

My father and I thundered down the hallway to the bathroom where something under the sink was making gagging and spurting sounds worthy of a medical emergency. Mom was in the doorway with both hands over her face.

"It's not a problem," I said, pushing past them and reaching for the faucet in the yellowed sink. "We replaced the water heater yesterday. It's just air bubbles in the pipes. We didn't have time to bleed the lines."

"Bleed?" my mother cried.

Dad, now crouched beside the bathtub, was digging under the linoleum with his Swiss army knife.

"Why this tub hasn't fallen through the floor, I'll never know! The wood is like butter." He stood and glared at me. "Whatever your slumlord is charging you for this pile of dreck he calls a house, it's too much. It's like a refugee camp in Africa. You are a middle-aged woman!" I cringed. "There is no excuse for you living like this."

"You could get a disease from the mold," my mother cried over his voice.

My father pointed at me. "Get your bathing suit."

I felt a spinning sensation as I often did with my parents. "Why would I need my bathing suit at just this moment?"

"You'll come with us to Hawaii. What's the name of this vacation package," he asked my mother, "'Lovely Maui Sunshine' or some goddamned thing?" My mother fumbled in her purse and withdrew glossy brochures. "You'll relax, you'll get a tan, and then you can come home with us and get out of this mess."

It took an hour of effort to soothe their concern. I refused the Hawaiian adventure, they refused tea out of fear the water might be contaminated, and they left, but the visit marked a turning point. Seen through their eyes, I realized the truth. Cringeworthy, certainly, and very real: I was a middle-aged woman with a secure job. I had a hefty nest egg to invest in a home of my own but I was living in squalor, afraid to leave my ragged safety net. I had no excuse. The metaphoric door was open. (The actual door was riddled with dry rot.)

Chapter Seven

"Why am I selling it? I haven't bought it yet."
—Me

It was serendipity. At the very moment my parents were railing about the bungalow, only a mile away a realtor was hammering a "For Sale" sign into the front yard of an adorable little yellow house. It would be perfect for me, with its artistically contrasting black shutters, shingles that appeared hand-hewn and, beneath a cherry tree, a ceramic birdbath with chubby angels. Jack could still ride his motorcycle over to see me every Tuesday and Friday. I had heard through the neighborhood grapevine that the homeowner was in jail, appealing a conviction for pedophilia—child sexual abuse—and he needed to raise cash in a hurry. True, that knowledge cast those chubby angels in a curious light, but even so, I hoped his well-deserved misfortune would tilt the asking price in my favor.

Jack had retired that year and was itching for a project, but he needed only one lap around the property to douse my excitement. "This yellow paint is hiding a shitload of problems. You think you have trouble with the bungalow? Wait until you're a homeowner with no landlord to call when the roof caves in."

"What could be wrong with it? It's delightful and charming."

"The delightful electricity is out of code and the charming plumbing is corroded. The east wall is out of plumb. These termites are probably the grandparents of your termites. You can get out of the bungalow. I'm surprised Earl hasn't paid you to leave. Try getting out of a mortgage because the cat pee is making you go blind. I can smell it from here. What were they doing in there, keeping a tiger?"

"Can't we fix the problems?"

"Yeah. 'We' can bulldoze the goddamn thing along with that sorry mess you live in and drop them both in a dumpster." Then he did a double-take at me. "You really want it?" I nodded. He sighed. "I guess it's worth about a hundred thou', tops. Offer 'em seventy-five. If they squeak, start talking about the problems. Don't buy it right away. Act cool. Make 'em sweat."

So, I called. A hearty-sounding woman answered the phone at the realtor's office.

"How much is that little yellow house with the bird bath?" I asked.

"Isn't that just a perfect little home?" she cried.

"Just. How much is it?"

"And what an ideal location!"

"Uh-huh. How much is it?"

"Now, there are one or two problems."

"I know. How much is it?"

"Four seventy-nine-nine."

What was this, some sort of real estate code? "Four seventy-nine-nine what?"

"Thousand dollars, sweetheart."

"Wait. What? Four hundred and seventy-nine thousand, comma, nine hundred dollars? We're talking about the yellow house with the bird bath?"

"Oh, honey. Once you remodel that place, you'll sell it for a fortune."

"Why am I selling it? I haven't bought it yet."

There was a moment of silence. Then she asked if I had an agent.

"What, I have to audition?"

"No, dear. A real estate agent."

"I thought you were a real estate agent."

"If you're in the market," she purred, "it's best if you work with your own agent. Now, what sort of house are you looking for?"

"The yellow house. With the bird bath."

We did a few more rounds and parted company.

Jack, who hadn't bought or sold property in years and didn't follow trends in real estate, was bewildered. Was the yellow house sitting on an unclaimed oil field? A diamond mine? Or, even more unthinkable, had he missed something? We went to look it over again. This time there was an addition to the "For Sale" sign. It was a banner reading, "In Escrow." In less than two weeks, the cottage had sold for what was evidently a king's ransom.

If Jack was mystified, I was energized. The sale of that cottage for that exorbitant price was one of those phenomena that would never be explained in my lifetime, like the moai on Easter Island or the reason my mother believed electricity could leak from the wall outlets. Now that I'd experienced a taste of freedom from the bungalow, I was determined to find a home of my own. This time Jack, for a change, was the fearful one of the two of us.

"Money isn't the only thing you need in your back pocket when you go out there to buy property. You were all set to buy that yellow disaster because the birdbath was cute. That real estate lady would have eaten you alive. They're worse than poker players. You won't see the dirty tricks coming until you've signed your life away."

"Other people buy houses all the time."

"Other people know what to look for and how to negotiate a sale. Look, I got nothing else to do and I know what I'm doing. You want to go house-hunting, I'll come with you. Jesus only knows what you'll end up with if you go out there alone, and then I'll have to hear about it."

So began our unwitting participation in a phenomenon that would make history. At that very time, property values across the nation were increasing by thousands of dollars every month, the subprime mortgage crisis was gathering steam, nefarious lenders were gutting the savings and trust of the nation, and soon the economy would teeter on the brink of collapse.

It was 2007.

Chapter Eight

"Who built this pile of crap?"
—Jack

Our forays began on Saturday mornings at the bungalow where Jack and I would be waiting for Marvin, my real estate agent. We'd hear the muffler on his ancient Cadillac before we would see him making his way up the road. After decades as a top realtor in the county, Marv cited me as his final project and would move to Montana to spend his days fishing once I was ensconced in my new home.

For a reason yet unknown to us, Jack and I quickly learned that the yellow cottage was not an anomaly. Property values had exploded. Even with my years of savings, my price range limited my house-hunting search to structures described as "needs some work," "a fixer with great potential," and "just wants some TLC." With Marv at the wheel, me riding shotgun and Jack stretched out on the velour-covered rear seat, we would spend hours jouncing over potholes and dodging guard dogs as we made our way along the back roads of the celebrated Northern California wine country, through the astronomically priced inventory of property that might, in another place and time, have been condemned.

Jack's presence was a mixed blessing. We would enter a home for sale. Marvin would begin his spiel, pointing out the crown molding. Soon I'd hear a snort from Jack. Then a moment of silence. Then the litany would begin.

"Who built this pile of crap?"

He would follow that rhetorical question with a list of fatal problems with the building's structure and MEP (mechanical, electrical, and plumbing systems), sprinkled with references to biological reproduction and elimination, often involving farm animals. After ten years I knew Jack's humor, his interests, his behavior in the kitchen and bedroom but this was my introduction to his work persona. His standards for excellence were worthy of an original Frank Lloyd Wright, but his communication about it could have come from an Alaskan fishing trawler. After one invective-studded diatribe that left Marv and the homeowner wide-eyed, I suggested that he not use so many bad words. "The homeowners are proud of their house," I said, "even if it is a pig's shithole."

He tried. "This home has some interesting features," he said on our next outing. He was smiling with his mouth but not his eyes. "I see you've ventilated the kitchen by shoving the motherf . . . the stove up against an open window." I braced myself as his voice became more strident. He leaned back against the counter but his attempt to appear casual didn't fool me. I saw him clench his fists. "Plus, you have an exposed gas line running across the garage floor. Nick it with a hot tail pipe and you blow yourself to fucking kingdom come."

He named each failed adventure. There was The Satanic Cult House where someone had painted a pentagram on a bedroom floor. Miss Kitty's Bordello with its red velvet wallpaper. Gone With The Sneeze, whose Southern-style wraparound porch was so infested with termites that we had to inch crab-like through the door. Ropes and poles suspended The Flying Wallenda Cottage over a creek.

After one stunningly bad day, I vowed to end my search forever. We had started in a small town along the Russian River which

a Version of the Truth

flows down from our surrounding hills. According to Jack, the area had been a popular vacation resort from the 1930s until the '60s. Wealthy families from San Francisco had built summer bungalows along the riverbanks but when the area's popularity waned in the 1970s with improved road conditions to Vegas and Reno, those cabins fell into disrepair. And now, those that were still standing were selling for the price of a small cattle ranch in Texas.

It was late on a Friday afternoon on that awful day when Marvin and Jack and I drove over a one-lane gravel road to see an "adorable rustic hideaway." I prayed that the Cadillac's shock absorbers would be equal to the challenge. The road wasn't the worst of it. The worst was the property itself, specifically the feature not mentioned in the glowing real estate blurb. That was the redwood tree growing through holes carved into the living room floor and roof. The tree wasn't even majestic. Its lower branches were yellowed, the upper limbs dry and barren. Someone had draped chicken wire over the hole in the floor, through which one could look down and see nuts, squirrel droppings, owl pellets, tree debris and leaves. We were among three potential buyers roaming through the place while the owner, a shirtless man wearing sunglasses and a straw hat, sat cross-legged on the kitchen table and watched in silence. Marv whispered that an offer had already been made and it was far above the asking price of $450,000. A bidding war might be on the horizon, he said. But the Tarzan Treehouse wasn't the low point of the day. That was our return to Bubba's Grand Estate.

It was one of the first sites we had viewed months ago, at the start of my search. The small frame house along the river had listed just within my price range for $420,000 and it was in terrible shape. A tarp covered the roof on one end and an old Sears-Roebuck air conditioner was perched on a ladder before a gap in the outer wall. A pit bull was licking his balls in the barren front yard where a man with a shelf of beer belly hanging over his belt was washing a pickup. "Looks like Bubba's getting his grand estate cleaned up for the Klan meeting," Jack had murmured. Even Marvin had known better than to stop. We had turned in the driveway and fled. Four months and a plethora of hovels and huts later, Marv mentioned a small frame house along the river. It was out of my price range at $480,000 but, he said, "worth a look." We pulled up to a structure that seemed oddly familiar. In the back seat, Jack was silent. I turned to see him wearing his most cynical smile. "Know where you are?" he asked. I looked again. It was Bubba's. Now a sheet of plywood boarded up the gap and an old television and bathtub were in the front yard. Since our first visit its sticker price had risen by $40,000.

My future was clear. I would remain a hostage of the bungalow until we collapsed in each other's arms. When Jack and I came home, I waited until Marvin left and then I cried, with Jack patting my back and looking demoralized.

Friends and family asked why I stayed in that overpriced, entitled little corner of the nation when I was mobile, childless, and could go wherever I wanted. There were two reasons. One was work. At my age, forging new territory elsewhere would have been unrealistic. Therapists are cutthroat and protective of their turf. The second reason was Jack. No, I needed to stay within commuting distance of my practice and Jack's commute to me.

Chapter Nine

"Three thousand tweakers can't be wrong."
—Jack

In April, 2008, the stock market crashed. Of course I heard about it. It had something to do with finance bros in New York who looked upset and yelled on the phone on the evening news. Why would I care about them? I might still be in the bungalow, covered in dust and mildew, were it not for a peculiar conversation with a coworker who explained why, in fact, I should have cared. I was at a table in the staff coffee break room with my head in my hands, fretting about the fuses that kept blowing in the bungalow. Jack said the entire panel was at risk for fire and someone with a state license would need to deal with it. Earl no longer returned my calls.

My coworker Benny dropped into a chair opposite mine.

"Rough time at the office?"

"Rough time at home."

Everyone at the office knew about the bungalow, but I had kept the property search to myself. I needed one place in my life that wasn't tinged with this futility. As I told Benny the tale, his sympathetic look changed to a quizzical one. "How come you don't check out Vineyard View?"

I knew the name. It was a railroad stop about forty miles out in the vineyards where trains delivered fertilizer and irrigation supplies for the big wineries like Gallo and Fetzer.

"People live in Vineyard View?"

"Are you kidding? Investors and builders discovered it during the housing boom in the early 2000s and swarmed like flies, tossing up everything from one-bedroom condos to gated estates with swimming pools. It was going to be the San Francisco of the North, with an equestrian park, a five-star hotel and a French chef. They even pimped out the animal feed store, turned it into a spa and tanning salon. Then a developer came in with a 'retirement community' for people aged 55 and over, not that anyone retires at 55, and things really took off. My wife and I moved up there in '04 so we paid top dollar, and we're mortgaged to the hilt, but we love Vineyard View. Just country enough to be casual, but not so country that it's scary. I hardly mind the commute."

"How come I never heard of it? My real estate guy dragged me all over creation."

"It was probably out of your price range before the crash, unless you're secretly Arab royalty or a dot.com hotshot when you're not working here. We barely made the down payment, even with us both working full-time and my wife's inheritance. Of course, it's all over now."

"What's all over?"

"Where have you been? The economy crashed."

"That loony business with the stock market? So what?"

"So real estate values crashed with it, is what. A lot of shaky mortgage schemes went down in flames along with the stock market. The developers cut their losses and hauled ass east to Idaho or somewhere. The fancy hotel site is just a pile of construction material now, and barbed wire to keep out the looters. It's like a ghost town, but with living people. You should look around up there. You might find a deal."

Jack was skeptical. "Vineyard View? Cow shit and meth labs. It's a notorious biker hangout, famous for having twenty bars and two churches. I think the town motto is, "Vineyard View. Three Thousand Tweakers Can't Be Wrong."

I cornered Benny the next day at work and recited Jack's dim perspective.

"That was the old days. I'm friends with the veterinarian in town. He said the housing boom changed everything. He could tell when the retirement development came to town and all the seniors moved in. He stopped seeing pit bulls with gunshot wounds and now he treats fuzzy little white dogs that eat at the table. Twenty bars and two churches might be an exaggeration, but the population flipped. I heard the bad guys moved up north with the pot growers."

Jack shrugged. "You've got nothing to lose but an 80-mile round trip." He scoffed. "Vineyard View! I can just see you with a shotgun and a Rottweiler who outweighs you, fending off the Hells Angels."

So, I went. The freeway offramp deposited me in a town that seemed to have been deserted by European and British settlers from the 1800s, and those settlers had upmarket tastes. Along the silent main thoroughfare, I saw faux lamp oil streetlights reminiscent of a Dickens novel, brickwork set in precise patterns after the iconic cobblestones in Paris, and a marble-fronted doorway with a silver handle that could have been lifted from a Spanish cathedral. An abandoned boutique bookstore sported a "For Sale" sign in the window and a dusty poster advertising *Eat, Pray, Love*. Just as Benny described, there was the reincarnated spa and tanning salon, once the feed store for cattle ranchers. The upper story still had wide Dutch doors for hay storage. The façade had been refreshed with gleaming white paint and accents of mauve and teal, probably not colors favored by cattle ranchers.

At the end of the street was a small coffee shop where several cars were parked, along with a few pricey-looking bicycles. No

Harley hogs with Hells Angels insignia, so I went in. The atmosphere was warm, fragrant with the aromas of coffee and pastry. Over in a corner was a varnished redwood slab coffee table, surrounded by people lounging in stuffed chairs and a long couch. The conversation was lively with frequent bursts of laughter and the group seemed approachable, so I took my coffee cup and a scone and found a seat. We introduced ourselves and soon I was once again telling my story.

One woman paid especially close attention. She seemed to be my mother's age, dressed like Anna Wintour of *Vogue Magazine* in a tailored skirt and short wool jacket with simple but elegant silver hoop earrings, a cuff bracelet and slender silver necklace. Eventually she reached over and handed me her business card: Edith Lovell, Real Estate. Agriculture, Residential, Business.

We talked until long after the others left. She was from an old local family, third generation realtors. "Don't give up and never settle," she said. I agreed to return the following Friday to dip my toe back into the house-hunting pool.

"Heads up," I told her. "I'll be accompanied by a construction worker who can pick apart a structure armed with nothing more than a toothpick and a flashlight. His language will singe your hair, and he'll find every flaw."

"A construction worker? In that case, I have a property you might find interesting."

This would prove to be an understatement.

Chapter Ten

"This place needs an exorcist."
—Me

On the following Friday afternoon, with Jack and me in the back seat of her Lexus LX, Edith parked before a sprawling one-story architectural structure—an oddly pleasing meld of angled lines, adobe clay, rounded doorways and hand-hewn shingles, part gingerbread and part Texas farmhouse.

"It's called 'Storybook Ranch,'" she said.

Jack commented that the roof was in good shape, a rare accolade, but I noted that the landscaping, although well-designed, seemed unkempt for property of this quality. Barren patches dotted the front lawn, hedges were overgrown, and a limp, clinging vine framed the front door. Strange signs of neglect aside, with a cursory glance I knew that the asking price for this property would verge on seven figures.

"And what's the bottom line for this little gem?" I asked Edith without trying to keep the sarcasm from my tone.

"Three hundred," she said.

It had been a hard-won education since the yellow house with the bird bath. I didn't need to ask, "three hundred what?" And for only three hundred thousand dollars, there would be a problem. Something structural, something environmental. Something

39

emotional. A sinkhole, a crack in the foundation. A murder. With one voice, Jack and I chorused, "What's wrong with it?"

"It just needs refinishing," Edith said. That's all she said. Then she opened the door.

We entered a spacious foyer with a high, arched doorway. Panoramic floor-to-ceiling windows framed an Olympic-sized swimming pool outside. It would have been inviting, had its water not been filmed by a layer of green slime. In the living room, where there should have been hardwood flooring or plush carpet, cream-colored walls met only bare plywood. The room opened to a kitchen that could have served as the staging area for a restaurant, but even from that distance I could see that the cabinet doors were missing. Gaping emptiness marked the spots where a range and oven had been. The lower cabinets were topped with more raw plywood that showed splotches of bonding adhesive, as if granite or marble countertops had been affixed and then removed. Bare planks in the center of the kitchen should have supported a butcher block island. Overhead, along the living room and extending to the kitchen, were rails for indirect track lighting, but they held no light bulbs. I saw no hinges, no knobs, no appliances, no fixtures.

This was not a home in the final stages of construction. Even I could tell. It had been finished and then gutted. An eerie, airless feeling hung in the room. The three of us stood, silent. I glanced at Edith, waiting for an explanation, but she was inspecting her manicure.

Jack spoke first. It wasn't the long "whooo . . ." that preceded ". . . built this pile of crap?" Like a detective entering a crime scene, he asked quietly, "what happened in here?"

"Vandalism," I supplied. "Drunk teenagers."

"Drunk teenagers don't have power tools," Jack countered. "This damage took strength, skill, time, and equipment."

Edith gave him an appraising glance. "You're both partly right. It was vandalism. But the vandals were the homeowners. Makes it worse to know they were real estate agents."

"The homeowners did this?" I asked. "And they were realtors? Are you shitting me?"

"Don't use bad words," Jack said. He turned to Edith. "What's going on?"

"Even realtors weren't immune to the feeding frenzy before the housing bubble burst. They used a subprime loan to buy a place way out of their price range. This one was nine hundred thousand."

"It depreciated by six hundred thousand dollars?" I was stunned.

"Not right away. First the economy tanked. The property owners couldn't sell overpriced real estate, even if it was their own, and they started missing their mortgage payments. They tried a bunch of different schemes to sell the place but eventually the bank seized it, and they lost everything. The bank put it back on the market at rock-bottom price to try and recoup some of their own losses."

"But why the destruction?" Jack asked.

"The homeowners may have lost everything, but they'd be damned if they'd let the bank have it. They ripped out whatever they could carry, sold it for scrap or dumped it in the landfill. This isn't the worst example. I've seen concrete poured into toilets, missing staircases, places stripped down, and all the goodies tossed into the backyard and set on fire. People are frightened and furious and broke."

I heard the familiar snort from Jack. "Well, we can't work with the fu . . . the mess they left us." His voice echoed around the empty room. The heavy stillness in the air was nearly palpable. "But the bones are good. For another hundred thousand, maybe one-fifty, we could take the drywall down to the studs, put in all new—"

"No." I stopped him. My skin crawled with the overarching feeling of wrongness. "Let's get out of here. This place doesn't need a remodel. This place needs an exorcist." Not to mention, I thought, carpenters, electricians, plumbers, architects, painters, all of the work and workers that would seem like a nostalgic visit to the past for Jack but that would probably overwhelm me. The crews and their supplies and expertise would be in addition to the shaman, priest and rabbi. I wouldn't have wanted to take any chances.

Chapter Eleven

"I can't find a damned thing wrong."
—Jack

Economy crash or not, Vineyard View was still a desirable corner of the nation and properties were still priced out of my reach or in need of repair—not due to age and deterioration but now at the hands of frustrated property owners in foreclosure. The Storybook Ranch wasn't the worst. We saw expletives spray-painted on interior walls in letters 15' high, once-breathtaking hardwood flooring left to soak under opened faucets, fixtures piled in once-luxurious backyards and set ablaze.

It was our tenth walk-through and a wintry late afternoon when Edith, Jack and I entered a tidy one-story home with a stucco exterior and west-facing windows that looked out over vineyards in the distance. The December sun in Northern California at that hour casts a unique sheen of rose gold and peach, and now it lit the rolling hills and a view of the river in the far distance. Without thinking, I felt an excitement that heralds the start of a love affair: hope mingled with fear.

Jack was uncharacteristically silent. He thumped on walls, crawled under sinks, flipped each light switch off and on. He felt around the windows, peered into and around appliances, examined the furnace and water heater. It was fully dark outside when we finished. There was no time to see the landscaping, but through the kitchen windows I could see what appeared to be a generous garden area and a redwood deck. Something about the house seemed to hold a nebulous quality of familial warmth. Jack opened the back door to peer outside.

"The deck is tilted," he said.

"Isn't that just the way with decks," Edith murmured. "I've never seen a deck that wasn't tilted."

"I don't mind," I said.

Jack shushed me. Then he turned to Edith. "Tell me something." She leaned against the kitchen counter and folded her arms. "This house was built just ten years ago, right?" She nodded. "And it's back on the market? This is a new house, in a desirable area, the previous owners haven't trashed it and I can't find a damned thing wrong."

"Maybe there's nothing wrong," I said.

Jack ignored me. "Did someone die in here? It's the law. You must disclose if there was a death within the last three years even if it was peaceful."

"It's OK," I interrupted. "Ghosts are OK." I could hear my heart thrumming in my ears.

"No one died, Jack," Edith said.

Jack simply waited, tapping one booted toe, gazing at Edith, head tilted, eyebrows raised.

"We don't typically reveal information about the homeowners," Edith said finally, "but this isn't a secret. They were in upper management at a tech startup in Silicon Valley. The startup failed and they were transferred to a parent company in Arizona. They're not happy about it but they'd be less happy with unemployment. Bottom line, they need to sell in a hurry."

Jack shook his head. "That's just the sob story they told you."

"I believe them," I said.

Jack gave me a knowing look. "Don't go getting riled up."

"I am not riled." I consciously slowed my breathing and tried to look bored.

"Before this lady (Jack jerked his thumb at me) gets any deeper into buyer's excitement and ends up with buyer's remorse, I want an official home inspection." (Edith reached for her purse and car keys.) "My friend Solly is a licensed inspector down in Corte Madera. I'll bring him up for a look next week and—"

"No," I interrupted. Jack and Edith did double-takes. "I want to make an offer."

Edith resumed her pose of casual attention. I wasn't fooled. I saw her pupils dilate.

"Are you fuc . . . kidding?" Jack asked. "It's a flashback to the Pedophile House With The Birdbath." Edith looked alarmed. "After all I have taught you, you want to buy a house almost sight-unseen?"

"I have seen it. You have seen it. I am weary and I want this house. There is no problem that can't be fixed."

"Well, there is one problem," Edith murmured. Uh-oh. "I believe there's another interested party."

Chapter Twelve

"I swear I didn't kill her."
—Me

Although I was never to meet Mrs. Francine Marie D'Artagnan in the flesh, I would always see her in my mind's eye as a character in a classic movie: cloaked in black taffeta and draping fur, with a lorgnette, pearls, and tiara—some combination of *Gone With The Wind* and *Amadeus*. From an internet search I learned she was 89 years old and came from one of the oldest and most wealthy of San Francisco families. She owned a Painted Lady, one of San Francisco's fabulous Victorian houses. Her personal chef had been featured in the "Home and Garden" section of the *San Francisco Sunday Chronicle*. I don't know what she wanted with a little house in Vineyard View. Hiding a family felon? Whatever her reason, Mrs. D'Artagnan toyed with me like a cat with a mouse.

I offered the homeowners their asking price. Mrs. D'Artagnan countered with $500 above. In a bidding war frenzy of anxiety and desire, I landed a scary financing scheme known as a bridge loan to offer $600 above. Mrs. D'Artagnan came in with $1,000.

I lost five pounds, and my mirrored image was gaunt. Even Jack was looking white around the eyes. Edith offered to reduce her commission for me. Jack and I were astonished. Her demeanor had always been like her signature silver jewelry, smooth and cool.

In the end it all came down to speed. I needed time to finalize the loan. The homeowners couldn't wait. Mrs. D'Artagnan paid cash. Once again, it was over.

As the new year came and went, I was in a fog of despair. Jack tried to keep my spirits up, but he was equally affected. We went back to pizza delivery and takeout Chinese. Meantime, that winter was especially taxing in the bungalow. When the deluges increased as they did in the rainy season, mildew spotted the windows as if ancient photographs were forming between myself and the world outside.

Living forces arrived in waves to take advantage of that outdated construction feature at the bungalow: the "pillar and post" that raised the structure off the ground. Access to the underside of the bungalow provided sanctuary for the rats, mice, raccoons, and whatever species claimed the creepy opossums with their serpentine tails. That year, the menagerie even appeared in my dreams, cavorting and dancing across the stage of my unconscious like Lewis Carroll characters.

Frogs had always been content to bed down under the eaves outside, but that January I opened a drawer in the bedroom and a frog leaped up, down, and out across the floor toward the kitchen. I never found it. One evening I noticed a potato bug trundling across the living room carpet. They were a source of cringing astonishment for me. I had never seen one in my travels elsewhere. The enormous insect's shiny brown carapace makes it look oily and its legs are attached on either side like oars, giving its walk a peculiar rocking motion. At my house creatures weren't killed simply because they creeped me out, but I couldn't bring myself to capture this one in a jar and find it a nice home outside. That would have meant approaching it. Instead, I went into the bedroom, stuffed towels under the door, and when I came out in the morning it was gone. Like the frog, I never saw it again.

And then on a Saturday morning in mid-February, Edith called.

"Are you still interested in that house with the tilted deck?"

I was too demoralized for teasing, or I would have reminded her that all decks were tilted.

"Why? I thought D'Artagnan paid cash and then I crashed and burned."

"She did pay cash. She moved in with a truckload of antique furniture and a wine cooler the size of a city bus. And then she died."

"She what?"

"She died. Tell Jack she didn't die in the house."

"Are you shitting me?"

I could hear the smile in her voice. "Don't say bad words. Her heirs put it back on the market this morning, but I wasn't going to list it until I talked to you."

To this day, when I tell the tale, listeners invariably ask me if I buried my Mrs. D'Artagnan poppet by the light of the moon. I swear I didn't kill her, by occult or any other force. Her obituary, a full column in the *San Francisco Chronicle*, said she had lost a swift but courageous battle with lung cancer.

When the dust settled and Edith gave me the key to that house, I had something in common with Mrs. Francine Marie D'Artagnan. We had both fought courageous battles, and we had both, at different times and in different ways, won and lost.

Jack and I celebrated with dinner at an upscale restaurant. My parents, friends, colleagues, and the Canadians were jubilant. Rachel couldn't pass up a chance to tease me.

"What, no more monthly home repair dramas from This Old Pile of Crap? I lost track of how many times your friend Jack replaced the Farnsworth Digression Switch that kept threatening to blow up the place."

"It was a Zinsco Panel, and it was just three times. Four."

"Five, but I'm thrilled for you."

I braced myself for a bittersweet move. At last, at long last, I would see the bungalow in my rearview mirror. But I'd also be leaving behind the relationship that had become, for all its quirks and mystery, a lynchpin in my life. Jack and I would still see one another but certainly not as frequently. Only forty miles would separate us, but that could mean an hour's drive up the freeway when the traffic was dense, not a mere motorcycle ride of minutes for Jack. I avoided discussing this seismic shift until his truck and my car were unloaded for the last time late on a Sunday afternoon. We stood in my new living room and surveyed the chaos.

"I guess I won't see you on Tuesday," I said.

"Why not?"

"You wouldn't want to come all the way back on Tuesday."

"Why not?"

"We can't get together like we always did."

"Why not?"

"You can't drive eighty miles round trip twice a week."

"Why not?"

"Because it's long, expensive and tedious."

"So what? I have nothing else to do. Your commute is almost as long."

My commute would be almost as long, but I was motivated by my career. In other words, money. But Jack? Granted, sex and food have been incentives for all species since the dawn of time, but I suspected the journey would soon prove wearisome.

Chapter Thirteen

"How would I get a cow to poop in my garden?"
—Me

Edith came by to see how I was faring on my first day as a homeowner. We sat at the kitchen table while I signed a mound of paperwork. Outside, the rain battered my quarter acre in a late-winter storm that had been drenching Northern California for days. Between the drama, the rain, and Jack's hovering concern, I had paid scant attention to the landscaping. Now, through the streaming window that overlooked the backyard, I saw a muddy swamp with frost-blackened branches, gnarled stumps, barren twigs and oddly, over in a far corner, a tangle of cables and wires. In my distracted state, I absently assumed it was a power generator in case the electricity failed, as if I were at a remote outpost in Alaska and not an hour north of San Francisco. Given the complexity of the documents before me, the possibility of managing an auxiliary power source seemed not entirely unreasonable.

"What are all those wires out there?" I asked Edith.

She squinted through the rain and then shrugged dismissively. "I think they're for the wisteria vines," she said. Later, I looked up wisteria on the internet. The flowers were pretty. If my wisteria needed a scary electrical substation, I could probably handle it.

Although Jack had hovered and seldom allowed me to finish an electrical project in the bungalow, I had some fragile grasp of how electricity worked.

Meantime, each Tuesday and Friday evening after I got home from work, I'd hear the rumble of Jack's diesel truck as he'd pull into my driveway from his trek up the freeway.

"This is ridiculous," I told him after the first month. "Come up here at noon. I'll leave lunch for you. Take a nap, sit in the garden, enjoy the amenities of life off the farm, like color TV and central heating, and I'll see you when I get home. Here's a key."

From then on, I would buy the groceries in advance and leave them for Jack so I wouldn't spend time shopping after work on nights when he was visiting. I'd come home to find dinner started and Jack asleep with the television on, in his treasured old recliner from the bungalow.

Then it was May. The rain stopped, the clouds dissipated, and the earth warmed. My dormant backyard exploded with blossoms, leaves and branches, shrubs and flowers and trees, insects and spiders and birds and lizards and snails. It was as if I'd suddenly become curator of an alien zoo, and all the creatures were either eating one another or eyeing me hungrily. If insects and arachnids and amphibians were already camping out, could fur-bearing creatures be far behind?

And all those wires and cables for the "wisteria vines?" They weren't electrical after all, although they gave me a shock of a different nature. They were supports and water lines for a vineyard. I can't fault Edith. From a distance, grape vines pruned down to stumps for the winter and seen through a rain-streaked window could be mistaken for wisteria vines. I wouldn't have known a grape vine from a palm tree. The fruit, at first the size of pinheads, eventually hung down on elegant shoots and tendrils like hundreds of tiny chandeliers, in hues ranging from deep purple to nearly pink. I would have been better prepared to cope with a voltage transformer.

Jack was out of his element in the garden. His mother did the gardening, he explained. He helped shell the peas she grew, and processed the tomatoes for sauce, climbed the peach and plum trees, canned and steamed and jarred the bounty. But the planting and growing? "The gardening stuff is woman's work," he said.

"It's *what?*"

"Up to a point," he added, apparently misinterpreting my expression of outrage. "She was good at stuff outside. She could whack the heads off the chickens, but when it came time to butcher the pig, she—"

"Oh my God, do not say another word. No chicken-whacking, no pig-butchering, and I'm about to whack someone else's head. *Woman's* work? That is the most outrageous, misogynistic thing I've ever heard . . ."

We tabled the issue, and I was on my own outdoors. Thankfully, a neighbor told me about a local gardener. Domingue had recently moved here from Mexico to live with his adult son and family, she said, and he was a gardening genius. She gave me his number and instructed me to leave a message with a time and day for his visit. His son would make sure he got the information. If he couldn't show up, his son would call. I surmised Domingue was too busy gardening to sit around waiting for phone calls and left a message for the son. Could Domingue please, please come to help me the next morning at 10?

Promptly at 10, a man pulled up in a pickup truck loaded with landscaping supplies. I pumped his hand and tried not to hug him. "Domingue, I am so glad to see you. I'm afraid I'm going to kill everything. I don't know how and when and what to water. Or fertilize. What is fertilizer, anyway? I just know it has something to do with cow poop. How would I get a cow to poop in my garden? There's a vineyard. I don't know how to make wine. And there's an insect out there the size of a four-year-old child. It keeps looking at me. I'm a nervous wreck. Can you help me?"

Domingue's smile was warm, and his eyes were kind. "No English," he said.

Somehow, during that long California growing season, I didn't cause Domingue an ulcer although he knew no English, I knew no Spanish, and when I'm anxious I tend to speak "like a jackhammer," I've been told. Then there's my stubborn Philadelphia accent. Domingue showed up every week and was calm and good-natured even though I plagued him with questions in whatever language I could summon or invent: semaphore, pantomime, exaggerated facial expressions. I did get a Spanish-English dictionary, but it added to the confusion. Once, evidently, I told him the cauliflower was eating my strawberries. (It was snails, *caracol*, not *coliflor*.) Domingue never laughed at me or seemed discouraged. If I had to work with me, I would be on anxiety medication.

After a visit to a local winery, I learned that my grapes were not meant for wine, thank God. Wine grapes need thick skin to aid in fermenting. But my "table grapes" with their thin skins and juicy pulp were perfect to eat right off the vine. I was absolved from operating a winery as well as a voltage transformer. Jack and I spent evenings after dinner that first autumn munching our way along the vines, debating ripeness and sweetness.

Chapter Fourteen

"The mountain lions come to our houses?"
—Me

My fear of the little furry animals that orbited the bungalow seemed comical in Vineyard View where the creatures were bigger, scarier, and virtually—sometimes literally—on my doorstep. I learned about their proximity one morning on a walk along a wooded trail near my house where I saw, thumbtacked to a fir tree, a hand-lettered sign: "Caution," it read, "Mountain lion sighted on path."

I arrived at the miniscule sheriff's office, trembling and out of breath. A young red-haired policeman sat at a desk doing the *New York Times* crossword puzzle. His name tag read "Sam."

"How many mountain lion attacks have there been around here, Sam?" I asked.

"Well, no humans have been attacked in recent memory but folks with little dogs learn the hard way not to leave Fifi outside at night. Or Fluffy, for that matter. House cats go missing all the time. When we're in a drought and the river and lake levels drop, a thirsty mountain lion can scale a 6' high fence for water in a backyard swimming pool. If they happen to come across a toy poodle snack, all the better."

"The mountain lions come to our houses?" I felt a trickle of sweat issue from my armpit and roll down my side.

He clicked a few keys on his computer and turned the screen for me to see a photo of a mountain lion lapping from a swimming pool. On the deck, one lawn chair was overturned, and towels were strewn as if flung aside in a panic. I probably imagined the blood.

"All sorts of varmints come to our houses," he went on, casually. "They got pushed back into the hills when the developers came. Then the economy tanked, the people left, the critters returned. It didn't take them long to learn that humans are a festival of tasty treats."

"Are we in danger?"

"Just don't walk alone in the woods and be sure you can run faster than the person you're walking with."

"That's not funny." (I tried not to smile.)

"Seriously, it's best not to hike too far by yourself. Do you have a big dog?"

"No." It wasn't the time to tell him I was afraid of dogs.

"Get one. A sick or injured mountain lion, if it can't hunt, might try to take down a person. They won't risk tackling a dog bigger than a breadbox. I'd loan you my setter, Rory, but then he won't come home. My wife won't let him sleep on the bed and he's always looking for better accommodations."

I noted this young man's intelligence, humor, and readiness to chat with a visitor. We talked for nearly an hour. He was a lifelong Vineyard View resident and had hoped to leave for brighter lights and bigger cities but discovered there was no work for someone with a master's degree in English literature, albeit from rarified Berkeley. From Sam I learned that, in addition to a plethora of wild animals, within a 20-mile radius of my home were 30 wineries. Their production ranged from 100 bottles a year at the boutique Icaria Creek, to as many as 400,000 cases annually at the Francis Ford Coppola vineyards. There was also Benny's retirement community, a Buddhist temple, an enclave of NRA gun collectors, a nudist colony, and ranchers and farmers whose families went back for generations.

When I got home from Sam's, I did an internet search. How many dangerous creatures roamed this area? In addition to mountain lions there were coyotes, bobcats, foxes, wild boar, skunks, weasels, and formerly domesticated hogs that had escaped generations ago, gone feral, and now were aggressive and could weigh up to 200 pounds. Small black bears were often sighted in and around the hills. From my perspective, no bear bigger than a chipmunk was "small." And since all mammals can carry rabies, I added bats to my list. Then there were flesh-eating birds—ospreys, vultures, eagles, and 13 species of hawks. The environment also hosted poisonous spiders, rattlesnakes, and a list of amphibians toxic enough to cause a rash on anyone unwise enough to handle one.

Jack was bemused. To him, one ate animals, rode them, employed them or ignored them.

"If you see an animal, don't put your hand in its mouth. What's the problem?"

"They know things. They have their own occult languages. They're always on the verge of something unpleasant to do with survival of the fittest."

"Every creature out there is more afraid of you than you are of it."

"Have we met? And why would Sam say I should get a dog for protection?"

"He's a policeman. It's his job to scare people."

Chapter Fifteen

"With my lousy luck, I'll live forever."
—Dad

The sea change in my relationship with Jack began in 2012 with my father's miscalculation. He was certain he would die before my mother. After all, his grandfather had died in Vladivostok at 45 and when he was twelve, his own father had died at 31 of an undiagnosed faulty heart valve. My mother's side of the family was known for longevity, with two nonagenarians and even, once, a centenarian. The odds were against him, Dad said. When I visited, Dad would make me sit with him and go over, once again, the preparations for my mother's care when he died. Mom would roll her eyes and say she could take care of herself. So I wasn't prepared for the phone call one afternoon at work. It was Dad.

"Hey, Dad. What's going on?"

"I can't wake your mother up."

"Is she taking a nap?" (Please tell me she's taking a nap.) I felt cold fear clutch my gut.

"No, she never got up this morning. I keep shaking her but she doesn't move."

"Dad! For Christ's sake, call 911!" I must have shouted. My coworkers rushed to my office door, wide-eyed.

Mom remained in a coma for four weeks. The doctors gave her no chance of regaining consciousness. At best, she would be "in a vegetative state" on a ventilator. I worked when I could and flew back and forth to Philly. I spent a week with Dad after we took her off life support and wanted to stay longer, but he sent me home. He remained ashen and stoic.

"Go back to work. I need to be alone."

Even through my own grief I pursued him by phone every evening and insisted upon his daily emails. If I didn't hear from him by noon, I'd panic. He simply maintained his nearly monosyllabic response. Yes, he was depressed but no, he was not interested in harming himself. Yes, he was able to eat and sleep. Yes, his friends and neighbors were in touch. No, he did not want me to visit him. "I don't need anyone hovering."

Finally, after months of haranguing, Dad agreed to visit me.

"I'm not moving there, I just want you to know that," he said. "I don't know what you California people have with trees. And I'm not leaving your mother." She was inurned in the Mikveh Israel Cemetery in Philadelphia. My father would join her in death when his time came, but "with my lousy luck, I'll live forever."

Dad was coming! I was in a frenzy of planning. We would drive out to the coast to see the Pacific Ocean, there was wine tasting and the redwood trees, dinner at local restaurants where he could sample the farm-to-table bounty. This was a tourist hotspot, and the options were plentiful.

"I know," Jack said. "Let's take him to that little restaurant out on Bodega Head for brunch. We could time it so we can get a window table and watch the fishing boats come in."

Let's? By now Jack and I had been "together" for over 25 years. On days when he wasn't with me, we talked on the phone and for the past few years during my annual vacation we had been treating ourselves to a three-day stay at a little motel out on the coast. While he was my anchor and companion, and he continued to make that journey to see me every Tuesday and Friday, we never included one another in family or social occasions. Now Jack wanted to meet my father? What would Dad, the articulate engineer, recent widower, bleeding-heart liberal, raucous celebrant of all noisy Jewish occasions, do in the company of this taciturn, conservative Norwegian? Dad knew about Jack, but I never imagined they would meet.

"I don't care what sort of relationship you have," my father said. "I just have one wish. Don't tell me about it."

And, if Jack was to join us, I was confronted with a wildly unexpected conundrum. My two-seater "Z" wouldn't accommodate two passengers. Jack's truck was also a two-seater unless I climbed into the truck bed and draped myself over a collection of auto and motorcycle parts. I would need to rent a car, but that meant a mind-numbing layer of complexity on the day of Dad's arrival. I would drive south to pick up Dad at the airport, take him home and introduce him to Jack. Then I would need to race north to the nearest Rent-A-Car agency before they closed, pick up a sedan and race home, an odyssey that could take as long as an hour.

The Rent-A-Car guy probably thought I was on drugs. For one awful moment at the counter, getting the key for a sedan, I forgot my address. It wasn't the moment to explain to him that anxiety can fog one's memory. I made it home, opened the front door and was horrified by the sound of my father, weeping. I flung my purse and keys to the floor and sprinted through the house to the kitchen, where I had left Dad still shaking hands with Jack. There, I found that the sound of my father's voice was laughter, not sorrow. "This guy," he said, jerking his thumb at Jack. "Can you believe he forgot to carry the three? Simple math on a blueprint and he nearly destroyed a house!"

"That's what I get for trying to add numbers in my head," Jack said. "It was when we were building that condominium . . ."

Jack joined us for a walk along the coast, dinners and lunches, and he and Dad hugged at the airport.

On the way home, Jack murmured, "your father had a rough time right after your mom passed."

"What? How do you know this?"

"He told me."

"My father told you?"

"He said he had a hard time getting his feet on the ground. It was like a bad dream."

"My father? That guy you just met?"

"Yes. We had a great talk. It was when you were getting the car."

"How long was I gone? Six years?"

"Well, your mom died the same month he lost his father."

"I never knew that!"

"And he said there was something about the way the air smelled when your mom passed. It took him back to that time of losing his father. The air smelled the same."

"I've known that man since before I was born, and he won't even tell me what he had for breakfast."

"I didn't want to ask, but I was wondering why he doesn't have those curls on each side of his head that Jewish men wear."

"Payot? That's a tradition for the most Orthodox of religious observers, the opposite of my father. Orthodox are the equivalent of . . ." I struggled to find a comparison and realized I didn't quite know what I was talking about. "The equivalent of Pentecostal Christians who speak in tongues."

"So what are you guys called?"

"We guys are called 'Reform.' We observe the High Holidays, but it's mostly about helping others." I could think of no better example of this practice, called *tikkun olam,* than my Canadian family. "For instance," I said, "my cousins in Toronto all volunteer in homeless shelters and take food to homebound families. They celebrate social justice wherever it happens, like at Passover in 1991 we had a special prayer of thanks that Nelson Mandela had been released from prison."

"You're kidding. Nelson Mandela is Jewish?"

"No, let me think of a better way to explain it . . ."

As we spoke, I formed a radical idea. The Canadian family grapevine had been buzzing. They refused to let more time pass before assuring themselves that Dad was OK. If he didn't show up in Toronto soon, nearly a dozen elderly sisters, aunts, uncles and cousins along with their children and grandchildren would descend upon him. It would be easier for him to come to them and he agreed . . . mostly, I assumed, in self-defense. And the best time for a family reunion was Passover, an annual event that was as much about eating and singing as it was about carrying on a centuries-old observance. It was two months in the future, but I was already packing. Consumed with work and home, I hadn't been to see my family in eight years.

"Jack," I said, "we're all getting together in Toronto for Passover in April. I'm going, and Dad will be there too. Come with me."

Chapter Sixteen

"So Jack, when are you two getting married?"
—Aunt Raysa

I remember one transformative moment from the Passover gathering. Twenty of us were seated around the big table. The air was heavy with traditional aromas of honey, herbs, red wine, fruit, soup and coffee. The seder had concluded. Jack had gamely read a passage from the Haggadah when it was his turn. We were sharing brisket, gefilte fish, and chicken soup. Conversation was raucous with laughter and debate and reminiscing. Then, during one of those curious lulls in a conversation, when for no planned reason everyone was simply quiet, my Aunt Raysa spoke. I couldn't see her, sitting in the middle of the row on my side, but I recognized her gravelly voice, cured with decades of smoking harsh Players cigarettes, a Canadian brand. Like them, Aunt Raysa was often described as having no filter. What came into her mind came out of her mouth, at greater and greater volume as her hearing diminished.

"So Jack," Aunt Raysa bellowed into the silence. "When are you two getting married?"

I choked on a matzoh ball. Dad, sitting across from me, sputtered into his soup. Jack didn't miss a beat. "Well, I can only speak for myself," he said, "and I sure won't be getting married again. You know how it is," he went on, conversationally. "You make a mistake in life, you learn from it, you move on."

Another beat of silence, and then Rachel cried, "the brisket is wonderful this year!" The chorus followed. "It melts in your mouth!" "Best brisket I've ever had!" "Never has there been such brisket!"

I loved the moment. Among the older generation, everyone—my father and his siblings and spouses—were looking wide-eyed or bewildered. They had married young after World War II, and remained married or were now widows and widowers. My seven first cousins, all of us Baby Boomers, were hiding smiles and attempting to cover up the awkward moment. We had forged the new relationship rules back in the hectic 1960s and '70s. Those of us who weren't in traditional marriages were in live-in heterosexual relationships, same-sex relationships, or dating, or were single, or were in some nameless place in between. And none of the children around the table, biological or guest or step or foster, seemed to register the incident. They were born into fluid and shifting relationship scenarios. And Jack was simply being true to himself.

Like a leaf blowing in the breeze, a thought drifted past my mind and caught there, shivering. I adored these people. I spent too little time with them. I was 68 years old. I'd had a long and productive career. It was time to slow down, focus more on my loved ones and less on my profession.

The week after we came home, I gathered my colleagues and told them I'd be retiring in a month. They gave me a wild party and some of us cried.

I'd had no plan for life in retirement other than to heft that "career woman" anchor from my identity and sink it down into my heart and home, but the first step seemed obvious. I had been taking Jack for granted. Lately I hardly noticed his presence, snoozing in that recliner when I came home from work. As well as being my confidante and companion, without his guidance I might have been vacuuming redwood bark and squirrel droppings from my living room carpet at the Tarzan Treehouse. The remedy came to me on my first week as a retiree when we were sharing lunch at noon, both of us feeling disoriented by the change in our schedule.

"Jack, you're retiring too," I said. "You've been working in the kitchen for all these years. It's time to hang up your chef's hat, relax, and let me do the cooking."

"Wait until I check the batteries in the smoke alarm."

"You may laugh—"

"Who's laughing?"

"But I have my mother's cookbooks, and the time, and the focus, and my mind is free from trauma stories."

"If you poison me, do I qualify for a trauma story?"

"We're off to a good start. You expect you'll live to tell the tale."

For the next few days, I used the internet to help me identify the accouterments in my kitchen. Some were from my parents' home, some simply accumulated over the years. I cried often, as I found myself reaching for the phone to call Mom. And I laughed. My mother's collection of recipes, hand-written on old index cards, told the story of her deep understanding of culinary arts. "Put pie in at 350. Don't let juices splash over when taking out." That was her recipe for apple pie.

The next Friday night, while Jack watched YouTube demos of guys in machine shops, I made real pasta sauce from my mother's recipe. I did almost as much Googling as stirring, learned what *sauté* really meant, took my time, cut no corners, used more than one pot, and it tasted like home. When he went back to his farm on Saturday morning, Jack asked for leftovers.

Chapter Seventeen

"This thing is a dog."
—Jack

Something was visiting my bird feeder at night, and it was not a bird. Every evening, I would replenish the supply of seeds and nuts for my songbirds. Every morning, the feeder would be depleted. Songbirds don't feed at night. No self-respecting owl would eat birdseed and no other birds feed after dusk. No rodent could reach the feeder. Some omnivore was out there, and it was stealthy.

I'd always been a light sleeper, awake at every sound even as a child, and especially sensitive now with the possible invasion of mountain lions, coyotes and wild boar. Yet, nothing was waking me. As a remedy, Jack fashioned an impromptu alarm: my wind chimes, attached with wire to the bird feeder. Any creature that disturbed the feeder would send the chimes pealing. I'd be wide-eyed in an instant.

The clock read 2 A.M. the next night when I heard the sound. Leaning up on one elbow, I peered out into the night. An animal, too large for a rat and too small for a lion, was standing on my deck's wooden railing, stretching up to nose the feeder. Its fur coat was silvery, limned by the light of a half-moon. I waited in the dark, breathless, staring from my window. After a few moments it slipped down and roamed my property, now hidden, barely visible, in and out of the shadows, silent. The night was too dark for me to see more than an outline, but while it was the size and length of a large house cat, even with my limited knowledge I knew it didn't move like a cat. It trotted, nose to the ground, head forward, darting more than gliding. Then it seemed to leap effortlessly to the top of my high wooden fence and was gone, leaving only the sound of my heartbeat thudding in my ears.

As a veteran of nature documentaries, I knew the rule of the naturalist: "Tracks are facts." True, animal tracks are typically read by David Attenborough or guys in camouflage gear from imprints in mud, sand, snow, or forest debris. At my house, they would be read by a nervous woman wearing pajamas, from a layer of flour she had spread on her deck under her bird feeder the previous night before she went to bed. At dawn, I was out there on my hands and knees in the flour where I found two clear paw-prints, each about the size of a quarter. I photographed them before the wind could carry them away and showed them to Jack the moment he arrived.

"This thing is a dog," he said.

"It's a *dog*? It can't be a dog. The fence is six feet high and locked. A dog couldn't have floated to the top of my fence like it did. It must be some sort of cat. Is it a baby mountain lion?" I fended off a mental image of a mountain lion growing fat on my sunflower seeds and casting a hungry eye toward me.

"I don't know whose dog, or what dog, or how it's getting in, but this is the print of a canid. Look at the heel pads. They have two lobes. A feline has three. Canines have these two large toe pads with small pads on each side. A feline has all four toes in a line. It's a dog."

Jack had been around wild animals all his life. He knew creatures and their signs but this time he was wrong. Nobody's dog could be visiting my property at night. Surely, although illogically, my fear of dogs would have sent me into a panic if a dog was outside my window at night. It was something else and I knew one person who would set Jack straight.

Sheriff Sam needed only a cursory glance. "Yup. It's a dog," he said. I was so astonished, I nearly forgot to be chagrined. "This is the pawprint of a California grey fox. It's probably a female, out foraging. She must have a den nearby. She might smell the birds that came to your feeder during the day, or maybe she's enjoying a quick snack of nuts and seeds. Usually they eat small birds, rodents and insects but they're not picky. They'll forage in your garbage if you let them. It's best to scare her away. She's not meant to be comfortable around people. Next thing you know, she's visiting the bird feeder of some hotshot who wants himself a fox-fur hat. For her own safety, she shouldn't be coming around."

"But I want to keep my bird feeder." In some nameless, subliminal way, I also wanted to keep the fox.

"Keep the feeder. You just want the fox to feel unwelcome. Get a dog."

There, he said it again.

Intrigued and fascinated, I read and watched everything I could find about my fox, her habits and behavior. Insomnia was my constant companion. I couldn't let a night go by without trying to experience, with some combination of fear and awe, the closeness of this wild creature, so remote and other-worldly. But Sam's repeated advice stayed with me. Get a dog. That year, 2016, was The Year Of The Monkey. For me, beginning with the fox, it would always be The Year Of The Dog.

Chapter Eighteen

"Oh good, you're getting a dog."
—Sheriff Sam

I faced a tundra of isolation in rural Vineyard View. Until I retired, I never realized how many of my work hours had involved socializing. Now, except for Jack's daily calls or visits, I often never spoke a word all day other than the occasional greeting to a store clerk or the mailman, and conversations with Rachel in Toronto. Although Benny and his wife had welcomed me to town, they were preoccupied with the social life typical of a married couple: Dinner parties, pickleball and wine tasting. Sam was always up for a chat, or needing help with a crossword puzzle, or ready with news and advice but he was two generations my junior and he was, after all, at "the office." My former colleagues and my friends from the bungalow days had made the trek up the freeway, admired my house and garden and never returned. Instead, they campaigned for me to visit them, in cities where we would find restaurants, theaters, and other signs of habitation. If I wanted to develop a social life in Vineyard View, perhaps Sam's unthinkable advice was my answer. I saw it in the scene framed in my living room window.

The parade began just after dawn with neighbors walking muscular, long-legged dogs. Their owners, in sweats and running shoes with their dogs beside them, jogged and trotted. Next, later in the morning, were middle-sized dogs and their owners, and just before noon would be the elderly neighbors with little yappy dogs. But as well as walking, the dog owners would stop to chat or would walk in pairs or groups. I never saw the dogs bite the people or one another.

Once I noticed them, I saw them everywhere in Vineyard View. Dogs in the hardware store where a "Dogs Permitted" sign was displayed on the front door beside bowls for water and treats, dogs in the bank, dogs in cars and trucks and I often noticed a young woman with a small German shepherd in the grocery store.

"I thought only service dogs were allowed where they sell food," I commented to Sam.

"Cody is a service dog," he said. "She's a Belgian Malinois. They look like German shepherds. When you think you see a small German shepherd with one of us sheriffs, it's a Malinois. Cody was an MWD, a military working dog. She and Allison were in Afghanistan together and they formed such a tight bond, the Marines let them go home together after Allison's tour of duty. Cody was 'in the service,' so the store manager agreed, she's a 'service dog.' I can't imagine anyone in Vineyard View ratting them out to the Board of Health."

Slowly, the concept took on form and texture. With a dog I could have a companion, protection from wild animals, a social facilitator. But a transition from cynophobe to dog owner would require planning, learning, consideration. True, a dog might not require as much skill as, say, a pet python or a buffalo, but how one acquires a dog, what they eat, how I would find one guaranteed to not bite me . . . the list of concerns seemed endless. Preparations and research would take months.

When I approached Jack with the possibility of having a warm dog to cuddle with us in bed on cold winter nights, perhaps a fluffy collie, he roared with laughter. "I can just hear my father," Jack crowed. "He'd say, 'Sure, hell, bring in the dog. While we're at it, why not invite the hog and a few goats?' And do you really want an animal in here, shedding and drooling and peeing on your nice carpet? Animals stay outside where they belong. Get a Doberman, a German shepherd, maybe even a Rottweiler or a Rhodesian Ridgeback. We'll get a puppy. I'm used to training hunting dogs, but it shouldn't be that much different to train a guard dog although I think you're pretty safe here. But no, the dog's job is to protect you and your house, not to cuddle with you in bed. Jesus."

Sam was at his desk reading *Best American Short Stories* when I stopped by to tell him I was considering his advice about dogs and I could use his direction. I emphasized "considering." Action was months, perhaps years in the future.

"Oh, good, you're getting a dog," Sam said. "There's someone you should know." He reached for his phone.

"Sam? Wait. Sam?" He looked up with raised eyebrows. "I've never had a dog."

"I know." He went back to scrolling.

"How do you know?"

"Because if you ever had a dog before, you would have a dog now."

This was no time for vanity. "Sam? I'm afraid of dogs."

"Why?"

"Because animals are unpredictable. And because dogs have big, shiny teeth and dogs can smell our fear."

As I said the words, a mental movie from my childhood scrolled past my inner vision. I was about four years old, on a Philadelphia sidewalk with my mother. A dog approached. My mother grasped my arm and hissed, "Don't look at it. It can smell our fear." I remember feeling puzzled. Fear? Comprehension dawned. "And my mother was afraid of dogs," I told Sam.

To Sam's credit, he simply nodded and went back to his phone. If my role and Sam's were reversed, I might have indulged in a few moments of probing about Sam's mother. He punched in a number on his phone. Someone answered.

"Hey, Caitlin, remember that lady I told you about? I'm sending her to meet you . . . Uh huh . . . OK." He turned to me. "Are you free on Saturday morning?"

"Why? What are you up to? I don't like this."

So that was how, on Saturday morning, I found myself in a room the size of an airplane hangar, surrounded by dozens of unleashed and uncaged dogs, with just a spray bottle of tap water to protect me from the shiny teeth.

Chapter Nineteen

"Aim for their neck."
—Caitlin

Sam would tell me only vague facts about Caitlin Riley and her project, Lucky Dog Rescue and Adoption. He said she used an unusual technique for matching abandoned and abused dogs with new owners. "Keep an open mind," he said.

"We'll just talk, right? I won't be around the dogs?" I wanted to surprise Jack with the news that I was looking for a dog, by myself, but it was too soon to tell him. Maybe in a few months.

Sam shrugged noncommittally.

I found the Lucky Dog site in an old warehouse on the far edge of town and warily made my way to a sign marked "Enter." So far, no dogs although I was aware of a cacophony of barking from somewhere inside. Caitlin's office was a confusion of castoff furniture, stacks of books, a large bag marked "Treats," a computer, food and water bowls for animals, and piles of dog-related accessories: Leashes, collars, beds and crates. Caitlin herself was a muscular, middle-aged woman of obvious Irish heritage given her name, red hair, green eyes and pale skin with a wash of freckles.

"Sam says you want to adopt a dog. What sort of dog are you looking for?"

"I'm not sure." Once again, this was not the time or place to admit I was afraid of dogs. "I never had a dog. I don't like the ones that bite or pee on carpets."

"Our dogs are housebroken and friendly."

Then she stood and motioned me to join her at a window set into the wall behind her desk. I walked over, looked through the glass, and for a moment couldn't make sense of the scene. The window looked out into a room the size of a high school gym. It was filled with scruffy couches, stuffed chairs, dog beds, dog bowls, dog toys. And dogs. Dozens of dogs. All dogs, roaming free. No cages. No crates. No fences, leashes, collars or restraints. The dogs were meandering, barking, romping, smelling one another or sleeping. A burly man with a long grey beard and braids lounged on a couch on the far side of the room, simply gazing out at the dogs while a younger man and a woman filled water bowls at a sink. They were surrounded by more dogs who stood in a semicircle quietly watching them. Except for the fact that all but three creatures were dogs, and many were smelling one another's behinds, this could have been coffee break at a conference.

Caitlin broke my hypnotized focus.

"Let's go in."

In where? Surely not in there, not in there with the dogs.

She walked over to the door that evidently led to the dog-filled room. I followed in anxiety-fueled disbelief.

"I'm going to open the door," she said. My stomach couldn't decide whether to sink into my bowels or rise into my throat. I felt sweat bead my forehead. "We'll go in and stand just inside for a moment." I could only gape at her. "The dogs will come to greet us. Don't look at them or touch them." If I could have organized my thoughts, I would have laughed in disbelief. Caitlin reached for a plastic spray bottle from a shelf nearby. "This is water," she said, and held it out to me. Somehow, I lifted my arm and opened my fingers to accept it. If I survived this experience, I would kill Sam.

I would probably get extra prison time for murdering a policeman, but I wouldn't care. "The dogs will want to smell you," Caitlin said, "but if any dog gets too close and you feel uncomfortable, spray it with water. Just aim for its neck. It won't hurt them, but it will tell them to give you some space. Then we'll walk across the room and sit on the couch with Roy. That's the man who looks like Willy Nelson and Santa Claus."

I could have refused. "Let me think about it and get back to you," I could have said. Or, "I just remembered, I left the (shower, oven, garden hose) running at home." A combination of ego and shock held me immobilized. I couldn't reveal my cowardice or gather my wits.

Caitlin opened the door just wide enough to let us enter. After she ushered me in, she closed it behind us. My stolen glance at the congregating dogs registered a sea of snouts, all pointing at me. The snout closest to the floor belonged to a dachshund, and the highest to a towering animal whose coat fell in long ringlets like dreadlocks. It could have been the offspring of a wolf and a llama. Its head, the end with teeth, could have reached my thigh. I resisted the urge to grasp Caitlin's hand and aimed my eyes for a spot somewhere near the ceiling. "Just walk casually," she said, and started out through the pack with an unhurried stride. I followed with my gaze riveted to the back of Caitlin's neck while I recited a silent internal mantra: *Jack would do it, Jack would do it.* Seen from this side of the window, that couch was farther away and receding. By the time we reached it, my palms, armpits, neck, scalp and feet were soaked with sweat, and I held the spray bottle in a death grip.

Caitlin introduced me to Roy, told him to take me back out in a half hour, and then wandered away. I sank into the couch beside him, but not quite in his lap. "Unclench, sweetheart," he said. I kept my gaze focused on the ceiling. "Open your palms, unfreeze your jaw. If you breathe up high in your chest like that, you'll hyperventilate and get dizzy."

"If I look at the dogs, will they attack me?"

"Don't stare into their eyes. But don't do that with any animal. A direct stare is a sign of aggression, just like with people. Glance at them in a friendly way. Go ahead." I glanced. "Not like that. That's a grimace. Just check them out for a moment. Then look at me, then back to them. Then you'll relax and they won't stand around wondering what the fuck is wrong with you. You look like a zombie."

"Can they smell my fear?"

"Yes. Animals can smell adrenalin. But almost everyone who comes in here for the first time feels anxious. Maybe not as much as you. The dogs are just curious about you. So am I."

It was wise of Sam not to describe Lucky Dog in advance. I would never have gone. And fortunate that I didn't know what awaited me. I would have told Jack. When I did, he was incredulous.

"You went into a room full of unleashed dogs? Hell, I wouldn't have had the guts."

Chapter Twenty

"We talk about you all the time."
—Sam

My first few visits to Lucky Dog were surreal. I kept returning, a combination of ego, disbelief, and intrigue. I couldn't let Jack, Sam, Caitlin and Roy know the depth and breadth of my terror, and couldn't believe I was surmounting it. I found the animals to be both mysterious and oddly familiar. I noticed it in the way they interacted with one another, the things they did, the ways they accepted and adapted. For my first few visits, I gave that spray bottle a workout. Any dog who came within an arm's length would be soaked. Eventually I could allow one to approach. Then I could touch, then pet one. Weeks later, Caitlin snapped a photo of me with the dachshund draped on the couch behind my neck like a boa, a mongrel nestled between me and Roy, and the wolf-llama creature (a sheepdog), gazing at me soulfully and drooling on my shoes. Lucky Dog became my social lifeline in my new post-career world.

Only hired staff were allowed to enter the "pack room" alone, and there were always three staff in attendance, so I'd begin my routine with a nod to Caitlin who was usually focused on paperwork or the phone. Then I'd grab a spray bottle, come to the window and wave to Roy. He'd stroll over to the door . . . there were never hurried movements in the pack room . . . and let me in. We'd chat there for a few moments in low tones as the dogs came to inspect me, then we would saunter to the couch.

Roy, with his ruddy cheeks, suspenders, long white beard and braids, was a Vietnam combat veteran, the second in command at Lucky Dog and a spinner of yarns. On lazy mornings I would join him and the others on the couches, surrounded by dogs, while Roy told us stories. Life before and after Vietnam, homelessness, heroin addiction, recovery, and dogs. Caitlin found him living in a dumpster behind the kennel and rescued him. Rescue was her mission, he said. And her method gave her a reputation beyond the narrow focus of the town and local dog aficionados.

"There's a theory," he said. "Creatures that get together in pack, pride, flock, herd, troupe, or school need a leader, an 'alpha.' Its personality shapes the group like a king or president affects a country. If the alpha is warlike, the subjects will be hoarding and aggressive. If the alpha is kind and even-tempered, the subjects will be sharing. The alpha keeps things under control," he said. At Lucky Dog Rescue, the humans are the alphas and the dogs instinctively act as deputies. An unruly dog gets a nip from a senior animal. "The dogs feel secure knowing a responsible leader is in charge," Roy said. "When they're allowed to come together naturally and sort themselves out, there's no need for cages or restraints."

I knew this theory. All therapists know the work of Dr. Robert Sapolski from Stanford University, the leader in stress response research. He studied baboons in Kenya and proved that when the troupe is destabilized because the alpha has died or is sick or injured, the other members experience a rise in their blood pressure and their behavior becomes unpredictable.

Roy said Caitlin was exquisitely attuned to each animal's temperament. "She knows how every one of them would vote if it had thumbs." He acknowledged that Lucky Dog was the subject of media criticism. One editorial opined that Caitlin's practice of housing dogs in an open pack was "an accident waiting to happen." However, her system had been working for nearly ten years and was being tried by other rescue groups. Some media-savvy folks with the same approach were making names for themselves on reality TV. They called themselves "dog whisperers" to reactions that ranged from outrage to applause.

I felt accepted at Lucky Dog, but I'd never be a "dog person" like Caitlin, Roy and the others. Their interaction with the animals seemed effortless, an almost psychic unspoken communication. I felt clumsy, an outlier, and I believed Caitlin could sense the difference. Sam disagreed.

"Caitlin likes you," he said when I had stopped by the sheriff's office with coffee and anecdotes.

"How do you know?"

"Oh, we talk about you all the time," he said cheerfully.

"You didn't tell her I was afraid of dogs. She had me in the pack room almost before I had a chance to take off my coat. I thought I'd die." I didn't add the part about wanting to kill him. His sense of humor might have had limits.

"You weren't afraid of dogs. You just thought you were." I glanced at him to see if he was joking but his demeanor was sincere. "You just needed someone to prove it to you. You had me fooled at first, but Caitlin could tell. It's her gift."

Chapter Twenty-One

"She was sure impressed with you."
—Roy

Dogs came and went at Lucky Dog, but I never met one I wanted to take home until one morning. Seen head-on, she was rail thin with ribs, hip bones and spine visible beneath a smooth, tan coat. She moved with a languid, almost feline grace. While the others congregated around the couch, snuffling and wagging, she stood apart and regarded me with liquid eyes that seemed especially large in such a narrow face. After the rest had drifted off or fell asleep, she glided to a spot before me and met my eyes for a long moment. Her gaze was cool and impassive. She could have been assessing a painting in a gallery. And then she snorted, turned, and flounced away on dainty paws and legs as slender as a ballerina's.

Roy exploded with laughter. "She was sure impressed with you," he said.

"What the hell was that?"

"That, my dear, was a professional athlete, a racing greyhound from the track in Tucson. The rescue folks from San Francisco got ten dogs out but only had room for nine."

"She thinks I'm trailer trash, but I think she's amazing. I almost wanted her to accept me. It's like high school all over again, but this time I'm the grownup."

"She'll be eligible for adoption in a few weeks."

"Like a regular dog? No way. A normal person could never give a professional greyhound enough exercise." In my mind's eye, almost out of my conscious awareness, I saw myself breathlessly running along the trail near my house with a dog, that dog, straining on her leash.

"Just the opposite. They're exhausted. They just want to sleep. The joke about greyhounds is that they make the worst watchdogs. The only threat to a burglar would be if the burglar trips over it. The dog you just met is Holly. Get to know her and see how you feel about adopting her."

It took several weeks of patient exposure but eventually I learned that Holly's flouncing, snorting and aloof demeanor were covers for a shy, disoriented, abused animal. In a distant way she reminded me of some of my clients whose tough, fierce demeanors were shields to disguise their own vulnerabilities. I could imagine her making a life with me. Jack had other ideas.

"No," he said. "Absolutely not. If you must have an animal in the house, get one of those fuzzy little white dogs. And a greyhound? Never. A greyhound is a hound. I know hounds. A hound is not a pet. A hound is a tool. She must work or she'll be high-strung. She'll bark and pee on everything."

"Well, you're being high-strung and barking right now. Go pee out in the yard and she'll feel right at home."

He shook his head. "You'll be sorry."

When Roy thought it was time, I bought the best dog food I could find and was waiting nervously by the window when he pulled up in his van and slid out, holding a large cardboard box. Holly trotted behind him. She looked larger than she had at the kennel. She could have been a calf. Roy had few instructions for either of us.

"Here's a bed for her, a leash, two bowls and five bananas. They're gifts from Caitlin. Feed her twice a day, walk her, pet her," he said. "If she does something wrong, simply say *no* and when she does it correctly, say *good dog* and give her a slice of banana. That was a treat at the racetrack, so she associates it with reward. Stay home with her tomorrow. Then whenever you leave, take her with you. She's been surrounded by dogs and people since she was born. She acts like she doesn't give a shit, but she'd be terrified of being alone. Bring her along to Lucky Dog to hang out." To Holly, he said "be a good dog." Then he left.

All day the first day, I tried to go about my usual chores in the house, but would turn to see Holly watching me, silently, not wagging or coming to see me, but standing or laying like the Sphinx with her front legs stretched forward and her head up. It was so unnerving, I called Roy.

"She keeps watching me. What does she want?"

"She wants to watch you. Stop trying to figure her out. You're a dog-owner now, not a therapist."

I slept fitfully for the next few nights and rose several times to find Holly curled in her bed with her eyes open. But she walked calmly on her leash and suffered with solemn forbearance the pats and admiration from neighbors.

I dreaded the next hurdle. Jack. What if she sensed his distaste for an animal in the house and became hostile? My heart was pounding when I heard his truck pull into the driveway. I would aim for a tone of calm authority. Cautiously, I opened the door. Jack stepped into the living room. For one breathless moment, he and Holly eyed one another. And then . . .

"Who is this adorable dog?" he cried. "Come here, sweetheart! You're a pretty dog! Yes, you are! Yes, you are!" Then he wanted to feed her and asked to hold her leash on our post-lunch walk.

Disdainful Holly was shy? Stern Jack was a pushover for a big-eyed hound? The woman with lifelong cynophobia was not afraid of dogs? Taken as a whole, this list of revelations made me wonder if there was anything else in life I could be missing.

Chapter Twenty-Two

"Nurses don't wear tinted glasses."
—Me

I had briefly met a few of Jack's friends in our early days together, and I knew nuanced details about them. This wasn't gossip, per se, but stories told over the years as humorous anecdotes or from concern. One of those friends was Barry. They had met in fourth grade, he was deeply religious, had a girlfriend who taught him to skydive, and his mom made the best strawberry pie. So, while I didn't recognize Barry's voice and wouldn't have known him if I'd passed him on the street, I knew his name when he called to say that Jack was in the hospital. He'd had a heart attack.

"Oh my God! Is he OK?"

"He has a stent in an artery and he's resting comfortably. He gave me your number and asked me to tell you not to come see him. He'll call you as soon as he's released."

Not see him? The drive to the hospital seemed endless. I thundered through the doors, barked his name at the front desk, found his room, dashed in, and vaguely noted a woman at his bedside, thumbing through a slick magazine. She wore a navy pantsuit, tinted aviator glasses and had short, red hair. I had only an instant to register her presence as Jack glanced up at me, his eyes widened, and then I heard activity at the nursing station outside his door. If there were sirens or bells, my mind didn't register the sound but suddenly, a phalanx of nurses burst into the room. One carried a stethoscope, one ran to the vital signs monitor, and one placed a firm hand on my bicep, ushered me out into the hallway and ran back into Jack's room. The incident took no more than thirty seconds.

I stood under the buzzing fluorescent lights, mortified and dizzy with confusion. I had come to comfort Jack. Instead, had my presence caused a medical crisis? Confidentiality laws would have prevented the nurses from telling me what had caused this drama. I could have lurked in the lobby to waylay the woman at his bedside, but to what end? My question, "Who are you and how do you know Jack," would probably have led to a predictable answer: "Who are *you*? And how do *you* know Jack?" In that moment, I wouldn't have found the words to reply.

Jack was released from the hospital and called me daily, but I didn't want a confrontation over the phone. Instead, I stewed and waited until he was well enough to resume our schedule, two weeks later.

"Ok," I said, once we were back at the kitchen table over tea and lunch, "what the hell happened when I came to see you?"

"You came to see me?"

"Don't gaslight me, Jack. Your blood pressure spiked into the stratosphere when I stepped into your room. What was so upsetting that it nearly killed you?"

"You're talking nonsense. What's this all about?"

"Jack. I walked into your room. A woman was there next to your bed. Then a flying wedge of nurses rushed in and kicked me out."

Jack furrowed his brow and shook his head. "I never saw you. I know some of the guys visited but I was zoned out most of the time."

"It was a woman. She had short, red hair and aviator glasses."

"You must have seen a nurse."

"Nurses don't wear tinted glasses. Nurses don't lounge around next to a patient's bed, reading *Vogue Magazine*. I want to know why you freaked out when I came into the room with you two."

"I'd remember something like that. I don't know what you saw."

Jack and I had always been forthright about our expectations. If he met another woman whose company he preferred, and she wanted an exclusive relationship, he would tell me, and we would part company. I was willing to accept his mysteries and quirks, but I didn't want to be "the other woman." It was clear I wouldn't learn anything more from him now, but the vignette remained in my awareness, like an incessant drumbeat off in the distance that was suddenly growing closer.

Meantime, the heart attack seemed to have taken a piece of him. One afternoon, midway through our traditional post-lunch walk with Holly, Jack asked to turn for home. "I'm sorry I got old on you," he said, and my heart flopped in my chest. Often, after dinner now, when I wanted to watch the sunset on the deck, he would simply rise from the table and call it a night. "I'm too tired this evening." I would follow him into the bedroom, wait as he undressed and climbed into bed. We'd kiss goodnight and then after watching the sunset I'd spend the evening at the computer or reading until sleep called to me.

Chapter Twenty-Three

"It was sudden and he wasn't in pain."
—The EMT

My father's passing was merciful. At 92, he was spry and quick-witted, ate and drank whatever he wanted, and still enjoyed a full night's sleep even after his customary cup of black coffee with dinner. When he didn't answer my morning call, I phoned his apartment manager and stayed on the line when they knocked on his door. He didn't respond, and we called 911. The EMTs estimated that the fatal heart attack had been about two hours earlier.

"It looks like he was having breakfast and just laid down on the table with his head on his arms like he fell asleep. It was sudden and he wasn't in pain."

The family members of his generation in Toronto and all of his friends had died or were too frail to travel by then. Rachel and her daughter had come to see him in the month before he died, and we agreed that everyone could gather in his honor in Toronto instead of making another journey. His inurnment was attended only by Jack and me, his landlord and several neighbors. I carried his ashes in our small processional to the spot where he would be laid to rest next to my mother's remains. It was Jack's first visit to the east coast, but we were too emotionally drained for sightseeing in Philadelphia and hurried home, Jack to the farm and me to Holly.

By then, many of my own friends were managing the demands of aging loved ones. They talked about their parents' and sometimes spouses' cognitive declines, dire diagnoses, financial woes and long-term care. I had been spared these obligatory concerns, but I wasn't exempt from worry. If Dad had been a young nonagenarian, Jack had become an increasingly frail septuagenarian. Chores and demands on the farm, which he had always met effortlessly, lately seemed to challenge and overwhelm him. While I was saddened to watch this diminishment in a man who tied his very identity to his competence and independence, I was eager to show some gratitude for his years of help, advice and expertise.

Some alternatives were simple. With the ongoing drought in Northern California, that old well at his farm had run dry and I could at least offer him water. While we all waited for the drought to end, he refilled gallon after gallon of containers with drinking water from my tap and showered at my house. I loaded my bath caddy with his preferred soap and shampoo.

Other remedies were more convoluted. His hearing had diminished, and talking on the phone had become an ordeal for him. One day, he needed information from Social Security but refused to call them. "They just mumble. You can't understand a word they're saying. They're probably all stoned." I called them on his behalf, and they apparently added my name and contact information to his file. I don't know what they wrote on the blank line for "relationship."

Then, when the fluorescent light in my kitchen burned out, I applied the art of the benevolent lie. A white lie gets you off the hook. A benevolent lie rescues someone else. Replacing the lights meant climbing a ladder to the ceiling. Jack would want to do the job but I feared what could happen if his foot slipped from the rung or he lost his balance. So, I told him that Drew, a local handyman, was in financial trouble. His wife had unexpectedly given birth to twins, I lied. (She'd been on fertility drugs for a year. The babies were possibly the most-sonogrammed fetuses in history.) I needed an excuse to slip Drew some money. Perhaps I could ask him to replace those fluorescent lights . . . The ruse worked. Drew scrambled up and down the ladder and Jack believed I had done a good deed.

There was Jack's monthly trek to the landfill site several miles from the farm to dispose of household debris. There was no curbside pickup, nor were there curbs, and he admitted that lately, the chore left him exhausted and drained. So instead, every Tuesday he'd add his small collection of refuse to mine for the garbage and recycle trucks on their Wednesday rounds.

These small alternatives were unobtrusive ways to help Jack age gracefully, I thought, and was blind to how dire the situation had become until the day I tried to phone him and got a recording telling me his number was no longer in service. With no way to contact him other than driving 40 miles to his farm, I was forced to wait until the next day when he would be with me. By the time his truck rumbled into my driveway, I was nearly in tears.

"Jack, I've been trying to call you since yesterday! I get a recording saying your number doesn't work. I've been frantic."

He shrugged. "Yeah, the damned phone's dead as a brick."

"But why was your phone service disconnected?"

"Some sort of bullshit. You can't understand what the fuck they're talking about."

Frustrated, I called AT&T. That was when I learned Jack hadn't paid his phone bill in over three months.

"Well, I get so goddamned many ads, my bills get lost in the shuffle," Jack said.

I felt a chill that began at my shoulders and raced in a frisson down my spine. What else was he forgetting? His medication? His doctor's appointments? Did he still have electricity at the farm? With wildfires ravaging the landscape, had he paid his fire insurance? I probed for details. He continued to insist that all was well.

"I'm an old geezer," he said. "I'm allowed to forget things once in a while."

I didn't know if he believed his own words or if it was too painful to admit that he was no longer managing his life as well as he once had. At a loss, with no connection to his family or friends and no role in his life that would allow me to call his doctor, I fabricated another band-aid remedy. His mail would go out more efficiently, I said, without meeting his eyes, if he'd send his bills from my house. It was a feeble effort and too desperate to qualify as a benevolent lie, but from then on, each Friday he would bring his mail along with his checkbook and stamps. It became a new routine. While he ate lunch at the kitchen table, I would open his bills, write the checks, he would sign them, I'd mail them from my box at the curb and dispose of the rest. If anyone had looked at my recycling material they would have wondered about the sudden influx of brochures from the NRA, magazines like *American Rifleman,* and the various Republican-tilted pleas.

When I went back to Toronto for visits, I never worried about Holly. She adored her pet-sitter. It was Jack who caused me anxiety. I fretted about him. We all did.

"Mazel tov that he's a genius with a hammer and saw," Rachel said, "but this is dangerous. Isn't there anything you can do?"

"If you think of something that hasn't already crossed my mind, please tell me."

My friends offered advice. "Just formally declare him as a domestic partner. You don't have to *say* that you only live together twice a week." As it turned out, I would indeed have to say. The rules were stern and formal. We would need to prove cohabitation for an entire tax year. Those who falsified their status committed more than a white lie. It was a misdemeanor and carried a stiff fine and possible incarceration. And Jack, who prided himself on meticulous honesty, would never have agreed.

Chapter Twenty-Four

"This isn't the time to run science experiments."
—Me

The crisis with the Ever Given, the massive container ship that plowed into the bank in the Suez Canal in March of 2021, felt like a metaphor for Jack's deteriorating health. A juggernaut on an inexorable path of destruction, slow, painful to see, impossible to change. On news broadcasts we were unable to look away as the ship ground itself into one bank and then swung around to lodge into the other. Jack's physical and mental decline seemed like a longer, slower disaster.

He now needed to urinate almost hourly, all night. The possibility of tripping over Holly or furniture in the dark and breaking a bone could be disastrous in a town so far from emergency medical care. An ambulance ride to the nearest hospital could take 30 minutes. So I left the lights on when he was with me. Sometimes I'd awaken to find he had not come back to bed. I would wander into the kitchen and see him sitting at the table with his head in his hands, silent and motionless, and Holly at his feet, gazing up at him. He would startle at my presence, seem confused, and then claim he had just come for a glass of water.

My bathroom became an impromptu drugstore with his bottles of pills lining the countertop. Often, he took them against medical advice.

"Why would I need to take my pills at different times of the day? I'm just taking them in the morning and I'll see what happens."

"Jack, the medical profession spends time and treasure on research. When they say to take your blood pressure medication at night or your cholesterol medication with meals, they have a reason. This isn't the time to run science experiments. It's your life."

He would agree, but still, I'd find yesterday's medication still in its bottle after he left.

Sometimes he would forget that he had called me and would call again. One Thursday at noon, I was turning the compost in a planting bed when I heard the rumble of his truck in my driveway. He thought it was Friday.

When he brought his checkbook but forgot his bills, brought his bills but forgot his checkbook, asked me three times to call his insurance company to make sure they received the payment for his bill, I tried to be patient, but this decline seemed more severe than what might be expected for a man still in his 70s. I feared these frightening signs. On the periphery of my awareness, I also began to dread his visits. I felt increasingly isolated and my trepidation was thickening and spreading across my awareness all day. Things could not go on this way.

As the incidents marking his deteriorating health seemed to increase and worsen, I pleaded with him. "Just tell me the name and number of someone in your family or a friend I can call for help. What if you fall while you're here? What if you have another heart attack? Tell me someone who can care for your animals and property if I need to take you to the hospital. I promise I won't call them unless it's necessary." He would vow to bring me a list, and then "forget."

Unlike that container ship, it seemed as if every sign of trouble would right itself. I lived in an ebbing and flowing state of false optimism. His strength would briefly seem to return, his cognitive ability would clear, I would convince myself that I was overreacting. Then his course would reverse and he would seem worse than before, one step forward and two back.

With these ever-growing issues, his safety and that of others could be at risk when he was behind the wheel of his truck and I insisted he phone me just before he left the house when he came to see me. My anxiety would rise with the passing minutes until he pulled into the driveway.

One day he admitted that he had been stopped by the highway patrol.

"They said I was driving too close to other cars, and I cut someone off on the freeway. They said they noticed me before. It's bullshit."

That was when, finally, I asked him to live with me. While I never wanted to cohabit as a condition of our relationship, I'd make the compromise if it meant keeping him safe. With him under my roof I could help him live his life. I needed to approach the idea with great delicacy.

"I have a confession to make, Jack," I offered over lunch, a time when he was the most relaxed. "I don't think you should be driving up here so much." He stopped chewing and glared at me. "I've thought of two options," I went on, pretending not to notice his expression. "You can just stay here with me, get off that damned freeway. I'll fix up the study so you can have a room of your own. It will be a win-win situation since I always need your help around the house." I didn't mention the ways he seemed to need my help.

He shook his head. "I can't just walk away from the farm."

"You won't be walking away. I'll take you back to check on things whenever you want." He shook his head.

"Then let me do the driving. I could pick you up at the farm at noon on Tuesday and Friday, bring you home the next morning."

"I'll think about it," he said.

"But, Jack . . ."

"End of discussion."

Then, one Sunday morning, another phone call. The man had that distinctive Northern California accent, harder to pin down than New York or Texas, but with inflections and jargon of its own. He introduced himself as Cliff. I knew from Jack's stories that, incredibly, these men approaching their 80th birthdays had been friends since kindergarten. He said Jack was in the hospital.

"Jack is in the hospital again? Is he OK? What's going on?"

"He had a stroke."

"Oh my God!"

"Yeah, he said you might be upset. He told me to hold my phone receiver away from my ear. But it's not a bad one. They called it by some weird initials, tee-something. He's OK and he's coming home tomorrow. But he wanted me to let you know."

No ill-advised race to the hospital this time, I needed direct help from an expert. While I might not know Jack's doctor, I did know my doctor. She had been seeing me for annual checkups for years. Since I seldom had a medical complaint, we talked about our gardens or our dogs. She knew all about my relationship with Jack. We joked about the required list of questions she needed to ask about my health and safety. She knew I didn't keep guns in the house and wasn't at risk for domestic violence. Was I practicing safe sex?

"Given the opportunity," I had said, and we both rolled our eyes and laughed.

Now I shelved all appropriate behavior and called her about Jack.

"Well," she said, "there's no such thing as a good stroke, but it sounds like he had a transient ischemic attack, a TIA. The effects are usually treatable." She gave me a rough idea of what to expect but ended with dire news. "Often, a TIA is a harbinger. There can be only slight damage, or none, but it is often a warning sign."

For the next three weeks after I spoke to my doctor, Jack and I struggled in our own ways. He became more forgetful, was withdrawn and lethargic. My concern for him seeped into every area of my life and often kept me awake at night. I would plead with him to stop driving, let me come for him or stay with me, and he would promise to consider . . . next week. When I'd hear his van rumble into my driveway, I would go out to meet him and walk him in, across the house and into bed, with his arm around my shoulder for support. There, he would watch television until I walked him to the kitchen for dinner. Sometimes he seemed to have difficulty not dozing over his meal. Now and then he seemed to rally, regain his sense of humor and interest in the world. Then he would falter again, and each turn seemed to take an ever darker course as his appetite flagged and he appeared gaunt and tired.

Like the hulking ship on its tragic course, something terrible was on the horizon and approaching.

Chapter Twenty-Five

(Stunned Silence)
—Me

And yet, when it happened, I was unprepared.

Jack didn't call me on Monday. As a veteran of our communication breakdowns—his answering machine was out of commission, he forgot, he fell asleep, he thought he called earlier—I experienced the silence as an annoyance with a slight overlay of anxiety.

On Tuesday, out in the garden, thinking of what to plant for spring, I kept my ears open for the diesel sound of his arrival. No traffic drove down my quiet street. When the sun reached its zenith, I went indoors to wait by the window. Shadows lengthened. Dusk fell. I shifted from anxiety to panic. This was my first sleepless night.

All through the next day, with my home silent, his phone unanswered and no one at my door, I waited and paced. Changed from pajamas to street clothes, showered and brushed my teeth, fed and walked Holly, changed again for bed and that was the limit of my ability to concentrate. I didn't eat.

The phone was my constant companion for the next three days. Since I was neither Jack's wife nor family member, the police would not have taken my missing person report, so I asked them for a wellness check. He was frail, I explained, and if he had fallen out in the pasture he could die of dehydration. They reported back. His farm was securely locked and there was no sign of foul play or mishap. Then I called the hospitals. Then the highway patrol, crisis clinics, every emergency and safety facility within a 50 mile radius. There was no record of his admission to a medical clinic, no accidents, no one reporting a man with his description. And then I called the psychiatric facilities. Then the morgues in all surrounding counties. They had no deceased male by Jack's name, nor a John Doe.

By the seventh day, panic had evolved into anger. He had kept me hidden all these years and now he could have died, and I might never know. Who would call me? Who even knew my name? With anger, I could afford a small measure of dark humor. I played out aggrieved images of seeing his obituary in the paper and then skulking in the back row of his standing-room-only memorial service, dressed in mourning, perhaps a veil, the mystery woman nobody knew. I would shock the audience, all those third-generation ranchers and farmers and mechanics, by rising to the microphone to reveal that for the past four decades their homeboy had been in a secret relationship with a Jewish psychotherapist from Philadelphia.

My friends and family were in a froth of concern. The incessant barrage of suggestions and speculation became chaotic. What I should do, what did I think happened, had I called the police, had he done this before, had I visited his haunts, called the hospitals, could he have run away, had he died somewhere. I knew there was genuine concern among my loved ones, but I suspected that some of my more distant acquaintances simply wanted to board the drama train. Finally, I told them all that I would let them know when I had concrete news. In the meantime, perhaps they would appeal to whatever deity they fancied and ask for Jack's protection.

Then I hit the internet. Among Jack's friends whose life stories I had heard, whom I felt I had known for years, I knew the last name of only one man, Dave. There was no route to him on Facebook. That was no surprise. These were men in their late 70s or 80s who probably had no interest in Facebook, if they knew it existed. With that option exhausted, I paid for a subscription to an internet service that offered addresses and phone numbers. There, I found five men in California with Dave's first and last name who were the right age. I didn't want to email. An email might have left me in limbo, awaiting a reply that might never have come. Winnowing through the list for a phone number, I found one slender thread and pulled. He lived in the area. I called and said I had been a neighbor and had been trying to reach Jack for almost two weeks. Could he help? The conversation was like tossing a pebble that caused a ripple that became a tidal wave and then a tsunami.

"It's been a total shit-show," he said. "The way I heard it, all of a sudden the poor bastard couldn't talk or move. Janet thought he was choking, but they weren't eating anything."

"Who?"

"Thank God, she got him to the ER in time. They said his fucking, 'scuse me, brain was bleeding. She was in a panic for the first few days trying to get the house ready for him to come home. She needed a hospital bed for the living room and she's having the first-floor bathroom remodeled for a wheelchair. He'll never use those stairs again."

There were no stairs at Jack's farm.

"She has a day nurse for him," he continued, "and someone to come in at night, but looks like taking care of him will be her life now. My mom had something like that happen."

I was somehow able to hear over the roaring in my ears.

"Janet wants to keep him at home for as long as she can," he said, "but they think there are some other things wrong with him too. Maybe the start of Alzheimer's."

I must have asked how to reach them, because I wrote down a phone number.

"Don't expect much from him," Dave said. "He can't talk right or hold the phone so Janet puts him on speaker and holds it for him. She can fill you in."

I'm not sure I thanked him. I do remember rushing to the bathroom to vomit. Then I called. She answered. Clearly my name rang no bells. I asked if I could talk to him. She said I could try.

"Johnny," she said, speaking slowly, "it's a lady who says she met you a long time ago."

Johnny?

I couldn't control the sarcasm or aggression in my tone. I asked, "How are you . . . *Johnny?*" His voice was thin and reedy, but it was Jack's voice, and he mumbled something incoherent and gave the phone back to her. She was polite and gracious, explained that he'd had a hemorrhagic stroke, his right side was paralyzed, his prognosis was poor, he would never regain his speech. She thanked me for my concern and expressed no interest in who I was or how I knew him.

How long had I stared at the wall after we ended the conversation? Everything seemed to be misplaced and misshapen. Like a car crash survivor, I wandered in a daze. He had never mentioned anyone named Janet. No one at all, much less a woman who would instantly assume the roles of wife, nursemaid, social worker and case manager. Nothing in our long association indicated that he was known by any name other than Jack. I handled his mail, I knew his finances. He survived on a carpenter's pension and social security. Who was footing the bill for day and night nursing care? Dave spoke of Janet's home as if Jack had always lived there. Had he ever actually lived at that farm?

For the first week, still in a haze of denial, I perversely enjoyed telling the tale. When my friends asked, "so, who's Janet?" I would offer a silent, elaborate shrug and then wait for their eyes to widen and their imaginations to run riot. Soon, anger, confusion and grief sunk their talons and I no longer used my story as fodder for a soap opera update. I questioned my sanity, bounced back and forth on the far ends of the emotional continuum between rage and bereavement.

Years of working as a therapist with trauma survivors gave me some insight into my roller-coaster of emotions. I hadn't been as traumatized as if I had survived combat, abuse, crime or disaster, but I was walking a knife edge. While my dreams weren't the recurring nightmares of post-traumatic stress disorder, I was sleeping only two or three hours a night. My senses were normal, they weren't the hallucinations that can plague trauma survivors. However, the aroma of a San Marzano sauce when I was cooking, or the sound of a country song from someone's car radio as it passed by, could prompt a cascade of memories that could deck me like an ocean wave. Then I would be lost in grief or anger, sometimes both.

Eventually I included only my two closest friends in updates. Neither was a therapist. I knew the temptation to analyze, probe, or advise and I didn't want to hear theories or answer speculation until I had climbed out of the abyss myself.

There were moments of humor along with the shock and distress as I pieced my way through the minefield of feelings. My confidantes, although unacquainted with one another, confessed to nearly identical concerns: Were they offering too much or too little solace? Should they prod for disclosures, offer to come and stay with me, open their home to me and the dog? Send flowers, wait in silence for my direction while fretting internally? "How am I doing with how you're doing?" one of those friends asked at one point, and we laughed. She and I had often shared anecdotes about our upbringing, hers in a Catholic family. Now she wondered, jokingly, if she should bring chicken soup, "Jewish penicillin," for my relief since I had no saints on board to hear my cries.

To everyone else, I said Jack was being cared for by family. Their opinion was universal. "You dodged a bullet," they all said. "He might have had the stroke when he was with you. Then what would you have done?"

Chapter Twenty-Six

"Yes, he does, yes."
—Janet

I lost my garden that spring. I planted, but nothing survived. The tomatoes I had planned to simmer with basil and red wine, to fill my freezer for winter, shriveled on the vine, still green. The seeds for my usual bounty of tender spinach, mesclun, and arugula, produced nothing but yellowed leaves, and my anticipated summer harvest of zucchini and squash gave me only spindly shoots. I knew the garden's failure wasn't my fault. Even as I punched the planting holes in the earth with my bare hands, I knew taking my emotions out on the soil didn't affect the seeds or tiny transplants. That would be illogical. And my tears hadn't salted the earth. It must be climate change, I assured myself. Yet, suspicions remained.

I called Janet through that spring and summer, ostensibly to ask about "Johnny" but more to listen for clues about her and their relationship. She told me nothing, and yet she told me everything.

"Does he have a good doctor?" I asked.

"Yes, he does, yes."

I heard it. Her voice, but Jack's language.

People in enduring relationships develop shared communication tics and speech habits that can only be forged over time.

They adopt one another's cadence, accents, anachronisms, pauses in common, the way Natives on isolated islands develop their own idiolect. Jack had a particularly unique speech habit. Ask him a yes or no question, and he would repeat the answer on each end of a sentence, like bookends. "Would you like a casserole for dinner tonight?" "Yes, I would, yes." Or, "Jack, have you seen Cliff lately?" "No, I haven't, no." Janet used that same linguistic quirk. So did I.

I heard him in her rare laughter, in her inflections, slang terms, and emphases. I spoke that language myself. It was as if we had been intimate friends for years, suspended over a chasm neither of us knew.

She never called me or asked for personal information but over time she disclosed more than language. I heard a devotion I hadn't known since my parents were alive. With my father, I saw it in the way he would carefully arrange my mother's morning medication on the kitchen counter, with a glass of orange juice at just the right temperature. I saw it in how my mother would forget which was her birthday and which was my father's and simply refer to "our birthday." Now I heard that exclusive tenderness from Janet. She housed, fed, bathed and medicated "Johnny," arranged for service providers, kept his appointments. She said she had taken him to the emergency room three times in one week to cope with hemorrhaging caused by a prostate cancer intervention that went awry. He had bled, she said, so profusely on the passenger seat of her car, that she needed to have it replaced.

The behavior I had attributed to normal aging was indeed the onset of Alzheimer's Disease and now it had been exacerbated by the stroke. He had become belligerent and even violent, a common tragic symptom of this form of dementia. In a rare moment of confidence between us, Janet said his verbal lashing-out had escalated. "The other night he put his hands around my throat. I'm afraid I'll die before he does. Or be killed."

My friend Eleanor, a critical care nurse, was explicit in her view that I had been spared months, possibly years of emotional, physical and financial challenges.

"Do you know what it takes to care for someone in his condition? That would have been your whole life, all your time and money," she said. "There's no escape unless you go into Witness Protection."

"You can't use Witness Protection to avoid someone," I said. "Only if they're trying to kill you." Even as the words left my lips, I realized I had unconsciously voiced the fear of my own fate, were it not for Janet. That could have been me, with Jack's hands around my throat as his dementia followed its tragic course.

Chapter Twenty-Seven

"You will never know the truth."
—A WISE FRIEND

As the months passed, I regained my footing after the shock and outrage, but the mystery continued to rob me of my sleep, hijack my appetite and muffle my love of life. *How had this happened?* Whether my answers were poetic or scientific or rooted in spirituality, as convoluted as a Homeric epic or pure rom-com tragicomedy, they always circled back to that single, four-word question. *How had this happened?*

Was Janet a version of me in high school, silently standing in the wings, pining away for her version of Jimmy Lee Bevins through all those lonely years, awaiting the opportunity which, impossibly, had come at last?

Was she a fantastically tolerant wife who never followed him on one of those Tuesday or Friday nights?

She wasn't a family member. Jack had no sisters or children, and his family was the opposite of my clan. From the anecdotes he told me, his people flung themselves as far away from one another as possible, never even exchanging Christmas cards.

Perhaps she was a family friend who belonged to a religious organization which provides hands-on aid to the suffering, and she was especially devout.

Or she was a fabulously wealthy widow, lonely amid her treasures, with the resources and commitment needed to take in a severely disabled man for no reason other than overflowing kindness.

Her internet footprint was sparse. A reverse phone number lookup gave me her last name, but I could find no mention of her on Facebook, LinkedIn or Google.

I could have called her up, sat her down, told her my tale of Jack and asked for her own, but I bore her no ill will. If they were married or in what she believed to be an exclusive relationship, I wouldn't risk causing her the shock and pain my story might have inflicted. Of course, there was also a practical danger. If I was "the other woman," she might have dumped him on my doorstep and peeled rubber out of my driveway.

And Jack. There would be no reckoning or confrontation or resolution with him. He was unreachable behind the wall of devastation that had taken his language and memory.

I needed the truth and only two people could offer it. One couldn't speak and the other couldn't know the question.

One day, on the phone with one of my confidantes, wandering again through that hall of mirrors and trotting out yet another list of possibilities, her blunt comment catapulted me back to solid ground.

"Listen to me," she said. (A long pause.) "You will never know the truth. So get a version you can live with, and live with it."

With that thunderclap, I realized that I was in a select group of almost everyone on earth. We live in a time when we're promised all the answers. If our standard resources don't deliver—our elders, clergy, professors, doctors and therapists—we can tap Google and AI. And yet, we still live with unsolvable mysteries. Some of us spend our lifetime searching for the truth. Some of us deny it. And some of us get a version we can live with, and we live with it.

I considered each choice in turn.

a Version of the Truth

What would it be like to press on, approach Janet despite the potential for harm? I could let my impulse and desire shout down my voice of reason. But it might have ended like a one-night stand: momentary gratification and, possibly, a lifetime of facing the consequences. Did I want to risk causing that damage? And to what end?

What about denial? Could I go on pretending that I never thought about this mystery again? When I was working with addicts, they were famous for resorting to denial in order to avoid addressing their addictions. A humorous quip we used was, "denial is not a river in Egypt." I might pretend, but that voice would still be there, clamoring for resolution.

When I'm asked for my version of the truth, and sometimes pressured to disclose it, I offer the only option I have: "You won't always get the truth you crave, but you can get a version you can live with, and you live with it."

I stopped calling Janet. When we last spoke, she had found placement for him in a memory care facility.

Chapter Twenty-Eight

(I wonder what I would say to him.)
—Me

I wonder what my life would be like today if I hadn't opened the door to that old bungalow, to let him in and follow him into worlds of risk I never would have known. I might have joined the other New Age Baby Boomers out to a soulless apartment in a city, to meander through the bookstores, spin philosophies, harbor my meaningless fears, and wonder why I always felt slightly out of place. Now, when I come home with my greyhound after our evening walk, I set up a trail camera out in my vineyard to capture the wild creatures that visit in the pre-dawn hours. A skunk waddles through, a band of rowdy raccoons, and my favorite: a family of foxes, a mother and two pups. In my mind's eye, sometimes on those evenings I see Jack in that old recliner, dozing with the television on, and I wonder what I would ask him, say to him. Then I walk past him and heat the oven for dinner.

About the Author

Marsh Rose is the author of two novels and numerous published creative nonfiction (CNF) stories and essays. She won first prize for CNF from New Millennium Writings in 2018 for her story, "False Memory," and was a winner in the June/July 2025 issue of Tulip Tree's "Wild Women" contest for her CNF story, "Dinosaur Rock." Marsh is currently a reader for *Hippocampus Magazine*. When *Boomer Café* was publishing online, she was a frequent guest columnist. She's a psychotherapist in private practice and lives in Northern California.

Her website is https://www.marshroseauthor.com.

www.ingramcontent.com/pod-product-compliance
Lightning Source LLC
Chambersburg PA
CBHW011254040426
42453CB00016B/2428